STARCODES

Also by
Heather Roan Robbins

Starcodes Astro Oracle:
A 56-Card Deck and Guideback

All of the above are available at your local
bookstore, or may be ordered by visiting:

Hay House USA: www.hayhouse.com®
Hay House Australia: www.hayhouse.com.au
Hay House UK: www.hayhouse.co.uk
Hay House India: www.hayhouse.co.in

* * *

STARCODES

Navigate Your Chart with
CHOICE-BASED Astrology

HEATHER ROAN ROBBINS

HAY HOUSE LLC
Carlsbad, California · New York City
London · Sydney · New Delhi

Published in the United States by: Hay House LLC: www.hayhouse.com®
Published in Australia by: Hay House Australia Pty. Ltd.: www.hayhouse.com.au
Published in the United Kingdom by: Hay House UK, Ltd.: www.hayhouse.co.uk
Published in India by: Hay House Publishers (India) Pvt Ltd: www.hayhouse.co.in

Cover design and interior design: Julie Davison
Interior illustrations on Chapter Openers: Lucas Lua de Souza
Interior photos on page 46 and 72: Shutterstock

Library of Congress Cataloging-in-Publication Data is on file

Tradepaper ISBN: 978-1-4019-7548-7
E-book ISBN: 978-1-4019-7549-4
Audiobook ISBN: 978-1-4019-7550-0

10 9 8 7 6 5 4 3 2 1
1st edition, June 2024

Printed in the United States of America

This product uses responsibly sourced papers and/or recycled materials. For more information, see www.hayhouse.com.

Your birth chart maps your soul's journey this lifetime, the wounds you're here to heal, the issues you need to explore. The potential is just waiting for you to joyfully tap it.

CONTENTS

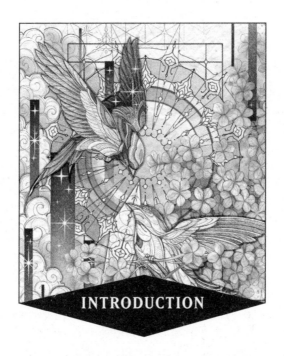

AN ASTROLOGICAL INVITATION

Come with me to this land of stars and planets, and bring your curiosity and doubts. I want you to try everything on for yourself, see how it works in your chart and life, look at the charts and lives of people you know and love, and let those lives teach you about this amazing system.

If you're reading this book, you are probably already on a path of exploration to know more about yourself and the nature of these beautiful universal patterns. You may have a longing to integrate Spirit and spirituality into your daily life. Astrology is a language of interrelations and interconnections that can feed that soul hunger.

Astrology is based on the concept that what we see above maps what happens below; we notice a relationship between the dance of the planets around our Sun and the energies we feel here on Earth.

Each of those planets symbolizes a personality, a multidimensional archetype that resonates throughout the world's mythologies as well as deep in our soul. They play out their archetypal dance in our lives. Stories of the Sun and Moon, Venus and Mars, Jupiter and Saturn, though they go by many names, echo through most every culture. The Greek and Roman versions are the most familiar and accessible, but each myth can deepen and broaden our understanding.

In this book I want to give you the lay of the land and help you learn how to read this beautiful map, to give you tools to begin your exploration and build a solid foundation. One of the best ways to take your astrological explorations further afterward is to read up on the planetary mythologies from around the world. I'll include some suggestions in the back of this book, under Resources.

The astrological signs act like filters on the world's stage lighting. The personality of each planet shines through the lens of a sign and takes on its tint and hue. The planetary personalities interact with each other in clear geometric patterns, or aspects; and so they argue, support, challenge, or energize one another.

When you were born, you imprinted the planetary pattern that was made at the moment you walked into this life. Those astrological patterns do not define your future, but they do describe a pulse or pattern for you to work with. You choose how you respond.

How does astrology work? Astrologers differ on their philosophies. I work with the theory that planets do not make you do anything; rather, they are influenced by the same pulse, the same universal patterns, that you are, and are easier to read.

Think of it this way: Imagine you're walking down a road along a fence, and you see sharp horns swaying over the top. You might not want to put your feet beneath that fence. The horns won't hurt your feet, but the hooves that might stomp your toes are being moved by the same great mysterious force that shifts those horns. The stars and planets dance above us, above the separation between us and the cosmos.

The planets are always moving through time and space. When you pop in, when you take your first breath, you imprint that moment of your birth, and the planets keep on moving. As the planets move, they set off harmonics, symphonies in your natal chart, and activate it, and you can choose how to respond. A map of your natal chart—your original pattern—shows where the planets are as they keep moving, how they could influence you, and helps you choose the best way to respond.

For example—and here we run ahead, just to give you a peek—imagine you have a meeting scheduled with a feisty ex-spouse and see that defensive Mars and electrifying Uranus are about to conjunct near your natal Moon. This is an astrological version of seeing sharp horns over the fence. It might be hard on your tender heart. Mars and Uranus won't start a fight between you, but they signal a pulse or pattern that could turn up the heat. Once you understand the symbolic meaning of Mars and Uranus, you can choose to direct this energy in a good way rather than have it ignite a fight. To work with this moment, you can choose to change a meeting date to a calmer time, and instead of wrangling that contentious gathering, you might head to the gym or launch a business and put that heat to good use.

These astrological patterns echo on all levels. They show the symbolic connection among us all. And importantly, they contain choice: choice among our interior metaphysical experience, the concrete realities of our everyday life, and the pulse of the practical, political, and mythic world around us.

ASTROLOGY AS A SPIRITUAL LANGUAGE

You may also become aware of an interesting subtle spiritual shift growing within you as you notice these symbols echoing on all levels of your life: how you spill your coffee or love your beloveds, what you see in political headlines, and how you experience your soul's progress.

What does it mean that you can track these astrological patterns in all these dimensions? Astrological symbols can only do this if indeed those levels are all interwoven. This points to a deep symbolic interconnection through all beings, all worlds, and all events. It is a flexible, hopeful connection—one shaped by both divine grace and our free will.

Astrology is one way that we can listen to Spirit, to those great universal patterns, and feel connected to the One. Each of us is a unique, independent being, and, at our core, we are all connected to all living beings, all our relations under the wide horizon of the sky.

My spouse, Wren, is a science educator and biologist who studied how cells use molecular symbols to communicate within their extracellular matrix. After long talks with Wren about how symbolism is a common thread in spirituality and biology, I work with this metaphor for consciousness, spiritual practice, and the astrological language that threads them all together.

One cellular symbol might say "grow," and each cell would interpret it according to its own nature, whether skin

4

or bone, arm or leg. To me, this is a wonderful metaphor for astrology. Venus says, "Beauty matters; lovingly create," and that is interpreted differently by an artist, a longing lover, a banker, a thief, or a compassionate caretaker.

We make our choices and activate different aspects of our charts, but that is not to say we have complete control. Our chart, choices, karma, guides and guardians, and physical realities interact with our extracellular matrix—in this case our culture, family, the politics and ecology of our world, and layers of generations of history, which is the soup we live in. All of these interact together to create our lives.

I perceive God/Goddess/Creator/Creation/the One—whatever name one wants to use—as made up of the consciousness of every cell and atom, every sentient being, working together; we are cells in the body of the One. That giant whole, that mega-consciousness, comprehends as much more than I do.

My reality as a separate individual is true; my choices affect the unfolding of my life. I have decisions to make and work to do; to deny my individual responsibility is to neither do my work nor take care of myself. Maybe I need to rest this lifetime; in some lives, we do. But I can't pretend I am a liver cell when I'm a skin cell. I have to honor what my talents are—and are not—and how I'm built and where I live to feel most fulfilled and be of most service.

But I am also a cell operating within the body of the One. I am a part of that Infinite. Information and energy flow to and from the core; we are not two.

Both realities are clear and true—my independent existence is real and so is the reality of my connection to the whole; it's just a perspective shift.

It's impractical and careless for me to pretend I am all spiritual and that Earthly things don't matter, and so get lost in my perception of Oneness. This can lead to spiritual bypassing and give me an excuse to skip my psychological work and practical responsibilities.

I need to honor that I am one cell in an organ—a symbol for the community of my family and culture—which operates within the body of the One. I need to do my personal work and take on the responsibility to help this matrix of my community be as healthy and functional possible, both for my benefit and the benefit of every cell within that organization, and as my contribution to the health of the One.

I can feel existentially lonely when I'm busy doing my work and feel stuck in the independent cell-mind of the daily grind. Spiritual pain can be defined as a sense of separation and isolation on any level. We feel spiritual support when we create connection, whether it is to one another, a cause, our guides and guardians, or all sentient beings. Spiritual practice of any form helps us mediate that flow and shift out of our solitary cell-mind and into the body of the One and our awareness of our connection to our Creator/Creation.

Astrology is a language of connection. It describes the rhythms of the universe and how they affect us, how our rhythms affect one another, and how we all have a place in this pulsing mandala of the world. It underlines the mystery that we are unique individuals and we are all one—part of the great whole, both at once.

CHOICE-BASED ASTROLOGY

The possibilities on your path are endless. Every astrological symbol of sign, aspect, house, and planet has a 180-degree spectrum of expression, from its terrible challenges, through its practicality to its divine gifts. These cycles are set in motion when you are born, and you can't change your chart or choose your transits. But once you understand the breadth of each symbol, you'll have a map to help you choose how to express that point. Your free will and your spiritual path interact with your astrological patterns and your world to weave your life's journey. That's where this work comes in. I want you to understand that there are 180 degrees of expression for each sign, planet, and aspect—nothing is set in stone—so you can make dynamic, healthy choices. The medicine, remedy, or empowering meaning for each difficult aspect and transit can be found in a positive expression of that same thing.

An axiom that gets this point across is: Your genius can be found in your bad habits, and your bad habits can be found in a problematic expression of your genius. The symbols for both your genius and bad habits can be found in the same places in your chart. What matters is how you choose to express those symbols.

For example, managerial skills, possibly from Saturn aspects, can help you make the trains run on time, but if not used well, those same skills can inspire you to become a manipulative bully. Organized conscientiousness, possibly a Saturn–Uranus interaction, can make you a brilliant scientist, editor, or manifester when you use it with clear purpose, or you can drift into rigidity or obsessiveness when you are under stress. Someone with difficult Mars aspects who's seen as a belligerent jerk can evolve into a wonderful hero who protects and defends, if they choose to use their Martian machismo for good. Astrology can point out the strengths of your chart and help you express them productively.

I don't intend to oversimplify here; we are all wired differently. As astrologers we need to be humble about the roles of karma and the effects of our extracellular matrix, our social ills, the gifts of privilege, and the challenges of systemic oppression. We must be careful never to use astrology to judge and say, "This is why you're miserable," "This is your problem," or "This is what you did in your last life." That is for the One to know. We are just cells studying a larger pattern. We can't say why you feel troubled, but we can give purpose, form, and potential remedies to that experience. Astrology can help you make the most of your unique skills and redirect difficult tendencies, but it works best when you combine it with personal introspection, good therapy when needed, and an understanding of your own nervous system. Let your chart be a map for that inner work. To become a great astrologer means to become a great person, because everything you see and read will be through the filter of your own experience, compassion, and sanity. Clear your lens. The wonderful, detailed universal patterns you'll learn to read will still be filtered through the depth of your understanding. So, have a life, and do your own personal exploration and therapy. Get to know people with an open heart and mind. Study world history and mythology. Study with a wide range of astrologers and astrological approaches. Look at astrology from every angle possible and see what works for you. And if you choose to take this astrological work seriously, make sure to apply that rigorous thinking with an open and connected heart. Do this work for the benefit of all sentient beings.

WHAT IS THE ZODIAC?

I see astrology as a wonderful and efficient symbolic map to help us know ourselves, navigate our lives, and make choices at a crossroads.

I wrote this book for my clients and all interested seekers. My goal is to make real astrology transparent and available to you, help you work with its powerful symbols, and give you a good foundation for any further investigations.

If you want to follow along in your chart, you'll need an accurate one calculated from your birth time, date, and place.

I recommend Astro.com, but many metaphysical bookstores, astrologers, and astrological websites can give you a hard copy of your chart to work with.

Don't be daunted by the complexities of the astrological language. Once you begin and continue, the lingo will be easy to grasp. The surface of astrology, our Sun signs, do give us real and solid information about how to deal with one another and yet float on the surface of a vast ocean of relationships and meaning. Your Sun sign is a valid place to start. Now look down another level, at the Moon and rising signs, and, when ready, spiral into the astrological houses and aspects to build out a more complex picture.

Once you start studying astrology, you'll notice that different astrologers have differing perspectives on the zodiac, house systems, and just about every other point. All these vantage points contribute another facet, another layer, to your understanding of the whole. Just know what system you're working within. To let you know my perspective, I was trained first in modern psychological astrology but incorporate mythic, evolutionary, and traditional astrology in my work and in this book. I work with the Koch house system in Western astrology, not Vedic or sidereal. So, let's explore.

So, what is a zodiac? Confusion about the nature of the zodiac is often used as grounds by non-astrologers to dismiss the whole field and can stir up trouble between Eastern and Western astrology. But the answer is actually pretty simple: the zodiac tells a good story and lays a solid foundation for your astrological understanding.

Let's look at the difference between the Western zodiac and the Vedic, or sidereal, zodiac.

There is no wrong way to look at the stars as long as you develop a consistent system that works for you and observe carefully. Like slicing an orange in different directions, each version gives you a different view and offers a most complete picture when we put them all together. The Western and Eastern sidereal zodiac systems conceive those "orange" sections differently but give them the same names, which is where the confusion lies.

The Western astrological traditions of Europe and the Mediterranean are Earth-centric. The zodiac is seen as a projection of the Earth, aura-like, radiating out from her body along the ecliptic. Visualize an infinitely flat and vast plane extending from the center of the Earth out through the Sun and all the planets. The Earth revolves around the Sun on this plane—though from our Earthly perspective, we see the Sun as the traveler.

The zodiac covers the band of sky traversed by the Sun on its yearly journey from the northernmost edge—the summer solstice point 23 degrees north of the ecliptic—through the equinox, when the Sun shines near the ecliptic, to the Sun's southernmost winter solstice point, 23 degrees south of the ecliptic. We divide this band into 12 segments or signs.

Once upon a time, when there were no electric lights to distract us, astrologers noticed a personality or inherent characteristics in each of these segments, and they put a symbolic essence of those characteristics into the signs. The position of any planet could now be measured by dropping an imaginary line from the planet down to the ecliptic.

Several thousand years ago (around 786 B.C.E.), on the first day of spring in the northern hemisphere, the Sun was visible against a collection of stars that we humans named Aries, the Ram. The sign Aries was named so not because the stars painted a clear picture of a male sheep (what do the stars know of sheep, anyway?) but because the energy of this first month after the spring equinox felt so brash and fresh, as boisterous and pushy as a ram, and so on through the 12 signs; our imagination projected symbols onto the Rorschach test of the skies.

Here lies a key, if unknowable, question. Which came first—did we name the sections of the sky after some quality of the constellations behind them, or did we name the constellations for the feelings and qualities inherent in that time of the Sun's cycle?

Slowly, over the last few thousand years, even the Sun has traveled through the galaxy. The spring equinox no longer occurs while the Sun is directly in front of the constellation Aries. The equinox wobbled forward about half a constellation.

Western astrology continues to anchor our zodiac with the equinox and solstices. Eastern Vedic astrology, used mainly in India and Tibet, along with Western sidereal astrology, follow the constellations themselves. Both systems keep the same names for the signs but mean different things by these same terms. This can be very confusing if you're a Libra in the west but a Virgo in the sidereal systems.

Both systems work within their own patterns, and if we weren't using the same names and meaning different periods of time and space, there would be no confusion, just different perspectives. The aspects between the planets stay the same and have similar meanings whatever system we use.

Some astrological skeptics point to a thirteenth constellation, Ophiuchus, the Serpent Bearer, to disprove astrology. Ophiuchus has a toehold on the ecliptic between the constellations of Scorpio and Sagittarius and has always been there. The constellations are of irregular shape: the Sun passes in front of the constellation Virgo for about six weeks but only spends about a week with the constellation Scorpio.

Because Western astrology divides the Sun's path into 12 equal sections, each 30 degrees, rather than following the constellations, we're not worried about Ophiuchus, nor do we worry about any other spare constellations. They are astounding and lovely and can give us extra information but aren't the point of this study. Any consistent way you look at this universe can give you information. The trick is to create a system, pay attention, and study the correlations carefully. Western astrology has been doing this (and due to additional research since the Industrial Revolution, we've added the outer planets) for about three thousand years. Back to that orange I talked about earlier: we may cut it in different directions, and each angle may produce different results, but it is still the same orange.

HOW TO USE THIS BOOK

You can read through this book like a novel. You can take this on as a student and use it as a workbook, responding to the embedded journal prompts that ask you to apply this material to your chart and life. Keep a file or journal with your responses and add tidbits and research you gather from other sources. Or you can use this as a reference book and look up what you're curious about when you have a question.

There is no wrong way. Astrology is spherical, a circle without a beginning and end. We learn the components to jump into the circle, then work round and round on this mandala to understand the deeper layers.

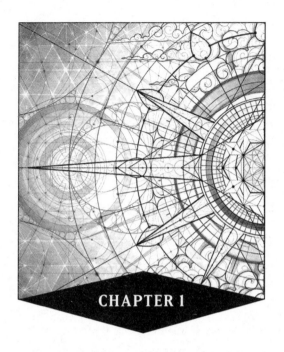

CHAPTER 1

YOUR NATAL CHART

Your birth chart is mandala, an interwoven quilt created through the interaction of all the planets, signs, houses, and aspects. No part of your chart acts independently of the whole. But to get started, study the pieces or patches on that quilt. Over time, or with an astrologer's help, you can weave all the pieces together into a coherent, useful whole, a beautiful star quilt of your potential.

If you do not have a copy of your chart, you can do an Internet search for "free astrological natal chart" and find many sources. Look at a few of them to see whose graphics seem most available to you, most transparent. I use Astro.com when I'm out of office—the astrologer's friend on the road—but there are many wonderful sources out there.

You don't have to try to understand your chart all at once—in fact, it's not possible. It is complex, a circle with no beginning and no ending. Start with the colors of the signs, then go into the planets and structure; you can take your understanding around and around in this circle, spiraling your understanding deeper with each layer. Most importantly, enjoy the journey.

First we'll introduce the signs and their qualities. Then we will move into the cast of characters: the planets, asteroids, and a few other astrological points of interest. Next we'll dive into the full astrological landscape, the cardinal points, and the houses where the planets dwell. From there we'll talk about the conversation between the planets and the aspects, and then cover the future influences of progressions and transits.

These astrological patterns were set in motion when you were born. Your birth moment can be seen as a culmination of your soul's choice and the patterns you began in other lives. This birth chart maps your soul's journey this lifetime, the wounds you're here to heal, the issues you need to explore. The potential is just waiting for you to joyfully tap it. You don't need to know the story of those other lives to see these patterns. But you might get hints of those unfinished issues that echo in this lifetime.

Your chart is not stuck in time. We take a snapshot of the planets from your point of birth; you imprint that moment and resonate with it, respond to it. It does not change, though your expression of it will evolve. You can think of this as your piano, your original musical instrument. The planets keep moving, and progressions and transits will play different music on that piano and bring out your unique symphonies over time. Now let's explore the signs.

THE SIGNS: FILTERS FOR YOUR LIGHTS

Think of lights on a stage, each one shining through a colored gel to create a unique space on that stage. The

Sun shines its light through blue or green, through Pisces or Taurus, and that filter colors its expression. Each planet reflects the Sun's light and shines its unique personalities through the filter of the sign it occupies as it cycles through the zodiac. In your natal chart, the signs light up the house or section of your life where they dwell.

You have every sign represented in your chart; even if you have no planets in the sign, it connects with a house and tints that field of your life. Scan your chart and write down what planets you have in Aries and what house begins with Aries or holds Aries within it. List each sign, which house it lives within, and what planets or points it contains, and let this be a quick reference as you work through this chapter.

Qualities of the Signs

Polarity, element, modality: Each sign is a unique combination of these qualities. Once you know and remember these qualities, it is easy to spot aspects and patterns without memorization.

Polarities

The signs alternate—yang to yin—around the zodiac. Signs of the same polarity have an easier line of communication and form the comfortable aspects of trines and sextiles with one another.

Yang: Fire and air signs are considered yang. Traditionally called "masculine," they are considered more extroverted and active as their energy reaches out. The signs look outward but may need help doing their inner work.

Yin: Earth and water signs are considered yin. Traditionally called "feminine," they are more introspective and may need help reaching out and engaging the world.

Elements

The zodiac begins with fiery Aries and rotates—fire, earth, air, water, in that order—through the zodiac. Planets in the same element are also in the same polarity and can form a comfortable trine with one another.

Fire: Ponder and journal on the nature of heat and fire. Think about the warmth of a fire in the center of the room where we all gather, the light that illuminates the dark and our hearts. Contemplate what might be too much fire—a spark can become a conflagration; a burning wildfire can take out a town. Contemplate a world without enough fire on a cold winter's night. What does the fire give you, and how can you use it with joy and safety? This range infuses all fire signs.

Fire signs: Aries, Leo, Sagittarius

Challenges: Fire signs can be impatient, self-centered, hasty, simplistic, impulsive, reckless, and incinerating. They can burn the house down!

Practical: They instigate, motivate, and infuse warmth and energy.

Gifts: As they grow, fire signs can be proactive, outgoing, enthusiastic, inspirational, energizing, direct, courageous, and warm. They shine. Look to your fire-sign planets and houses for the originating spark and for energy and warmth.

Earth: Ponder and journal on the nature of Earth and this material world. Think about your body, your Earth, the ground around you, the possessions you own, the trees in the garden, and the depth of a canyon. What strength and grounding does the element of Earth give you? What does it feel like when there is too much Earth—when you feel its heaviness, or feel crowded or stuck in a cave? Where there isn't enough Earth, do you feel ungrounded, unsupported? These qualities infuse the earth signs.

Earth signs: Taurus, Virgo, Capricorn

Challenges: Earth signs can be rooted, stubborn, resistant to change, and materialistic. They nudge us to need to see it to believe it. They can be hungry and focused on the senses.

Practical: Earth signs infuse common sense, grounding, building, endurance, and solid effort. They can help us manifest and create a vessel for all other work.

Gifts: Balanced earth signs help us birth a sacred form and embody the spirit. They can stabilize us and bring an Earthy, practical sensuality. They feed us. Look to your Earth sign, the planets, and the houses for tools to embody, manifest, and make it so.

Air: Explore the nature of air. What is the gift of a fresh breeze, of room to breathe? How do you experience the gift of the air with birdsong echoing on the balmy spring winds across a wide horizon? Consider the danger of air when there's too much in a howling storm or too little in a stale, closed room. Take a full breath. These qualities infuse the air signs.

Air signs: Gemini, Libra, Aquarius

Challenges: Air signs can leave us spacey, disconnected, impractical, stuck in the mind and its philosophies, glib or facile, or lost in fantasy.

Practical: They offer spaciousness, openness, articulation, and intelligence, and encourage communication and a more dispassionate overview. They naturally network and form community connections.

Gifts: As they mature, air signs can bring a thoughtful, interpersonal, and inspired perspective—a hawk's-eye view, seeing far horizons and the breath of Spirit. Look to your air-sign houses and planets to learn and express.

Water: Ponder and take notes about the nature of water. How good does a glass of water taste, what brings tears, what affects the rivers? How can you flow around obstacles like a stream? What are your oceanic, unplumbed depths? What does it feel like to be flooded and have too much water versus what is it like to be dry in a desert? These qualities infuse the water signs.

Water signs: Cancer, Scorpio, Pisces

Challenges: Water signs can bring hypersensitivity, become emotionally labile, have a fluid sense of self, and be reactive, defensive, and easily flooded.

Practical: They can impart emotional intelligence, perception, sensitivity, imagination, and empathy.

Gifts: When developed they call us to oceanic depth, sensitive introspection, compassion, imagination, and heart-centered intuition. Look to your water-sign houses and planets to deepen your perception.

Modality

A sign's modality describes its place in the beginning, middle, or the end of a season. Signs in the same modality form challenging squares or oppositions to one another.

Cardinal: Aries, Cancer, Libra, and Capricorn. Every season begins with a cardinal sign. They get the party started and can see what needs to be done. They may lack follow-through but can initiate and lead their element. Look to your cardinal-sign planets and houses to begin and explore.

Fixed: Taurus, Leo, Scorpio, and Aquarius. A fixed sign is smack in the middle of the season, when it's very clear from the weather what season it is. Fixed signs infuse stability and stubbornness. They help us continue and follow through. Look to your fixed-sign planets and houses to hold steady, root, and stabilize.

Mutable: Gemini, Virgo, Sagittarius, and Pisces. Mutable signs finish the season as the weather begins to change; one minute it's spring, the next summer, then back to spring. Mutable signs are changeable and may be hard to pin down but loan versatility, adaptability, and the ability to relate. Look to your mutable planets and houses to adjust, adapt, and express.

How do you feel at the beginning of the season, in the middle at the cross-quarter days, or at the end of the season as the weather changes? Notice the modalities represented in your chart—do you have more planets and points in cardinal, fixed, or mutable?

Balance

The soul longs for balance and completion. If you are low on a quality, you may be drawn to people who shine with it or reach for experiences that stretch you in that direction. If you are low on Earth in your chart and feel ungrounded, for example, you may find it helpful to spend time outside gardening or dealing with practical matters or with Earthy, practical friends until that side of you feels stronger. If you are low on water, life may call you to deal with other people's feelings, learn compassion, and be patiently present for other people's hearts. If you are low on air, education helps develop your thinking process and helps you express your natural brilliance in a verbal form. If you are low on fire, you may draw in fiery personalities or need intense motivation to begin new things, and so learn to be inspired.

Are there gaps in your chart? What modality or elements are underrepresented? Think about how you bring these elements in through your experience and friendships.

The Signs' Rulers

Rulership: Each sign has a planetary ruler, a planet that acts as the head of its household. You can look at the condition of that planet—check out what house it is in, whether it's in a sign that makes it happy or stretches it uncomfortably, and what aspects it makes to other planets—for extra layers of information about how that sign operates in your chart. Some signs have two rulers, both a traditional planetary ruler, one of the planets able to be seen by the naked eye, and a modern ruler only seen through a telescope. Astrologers differ on their techniques with rulership; I find the traditional, visible rulers work best when I am investigating practical, concrete, observable events, and the modern rulers add the more metaphysical undertones.

Astrological Signs			Aspects	
♈ Aries	♉ Taurus	♊ Gemini	♂	Conjunction
♋ Cancer	♌ Leo	♍ Virgo	♊	Opposition
♎ Libra	♏ Scorpio	♐ Sagittarius	△	Trine
♑ Capricorn	♒ Aquarius	♓ Pisces	□	Square
Planets			⊻	Semi-sextile
			✶	Sextile
☉ Sun	☽ Moon	☿ Mercury	⊼	Inconjunct
♀ Venus	♂ Mars	♃ Jupiter	∠	Semi-square
♄ Saturn	♅ Uranus	♆ Neptune	⊡	Sesqui-quadrate
♇ Pluto	☊ North Node	☋ South Node	✳	Septile
⚷ Chiron	⚴ Pallas	⚵ Juno	⋈	Novile
⚳ Ceres	⚶ Vesta	⊕ Earth		

Above is a key to the graphic symbols in your chart so you can follow along as we move forward in exploring your inner landscape.

CHAPTER 2

LENSES FOR YOUR LIGHTS: THE SIGNS

Before we move through the astrological signs, a note on dates: the signs change approximately on the 21st of each month, but this can vary to somewhere between the 18th and the 23rd, depending on the year and month.

ARIES—ACTIVATE

The Sun shines through Aries from approximately March 20 to April 20. Aries is ruled by Mars. It is a cardinal fire sign, the leader of the fire signs, whose fresh, brash enthusiasm is symbolized by a headstrong ram. As the Sun enters Aries, it asks us to remember our fire, our personal reasons for being alive, and pumps up the volume on will and life force. Aries energy is raw, exhilarated, direct, rude, and passionate and looking for a challenge. Aries governs the head and infuses the capacity for initiation, new beginnings, spontaneity, rebellion, and rebirth.

Challenge: Headstrong, unsubtle Aries can imbue a knee-jerk pugnacious or rebellious response, a compulsively oppositional approach wherever it sits in our chart. Watch for that Aries tendency to act first and think later, a "ready, fire, aim" mentality that ignites an argument or accident. Here you may be uncomfortable showing weakness or taking direction. You can get bored easily and start trouble or go off in search of the next challenge. Or you can feel you need to be strong and therefore endure something that should not be endured. Here you are challenged not to be easily sidetracked in rebellion and reaction but to stay on track—your track—toward your purpose. If you find yourself too hot to handle, redirect.

Practical: Think of a plant with the guts to come back alive after a long, hard winter. Aries loves fresh territory, gets bored with repetition, and has no tolerance for trivia. Where you have Aries, you rarely take the easy route. Aries brings resistance, rebellion, and acts of pure will. It loans the courage to begin again; to be direct, brave, and exploratory; and to lead, whether others like it or not. Here you are willing to forge new paths. You can engage entrepreneurship, adventure, competition, athleticism, martial arts, or any of our culturally macho elements. You may have trouble taking advice or direction, but if you can find something to respect in the competency and strength of another, you can learn from or follow them.

Gift: You slice through the dross and cut to the chase, strong and ready speak your mind. Your Aries encourages you to boldly go where you have not gone before. Here you can be straightforward, honest, and direct and support others. Aries imbues the strength and courage to take on a challenge and throw off an oppressive situation. Where you have Aries, you can find your own way and hear your own inner calling. Here you start over and have the guts to build from scratch. With added mature thoughtfulness, Aries inspires healthy leadership.

Nurture: Practice planned spontaneity: work into your schedule a few hours or days where you can do whatever you feel like at the time, without preplanning or having to coordinate with anyone else. Drive down the road and see which way the car turns; walk and see where your feet take you. Start painting and see what the brush creates. Meander and imagine how you'd solve a problem if you didn't have to make any compromises. It may take a while to unwind from external pressures and listen for that source within, but when you get a chance, that creative vitality can geyser up from the depths and help you come back alive. When you reengage, you'll feel more energized, less explosive, and able to compromise without losing your vision.

TAURUS—CULTIVATE

The Sun walks through Taurus from approximately April 21 to May 20. Fixed-Earth Taurus brings the Aries fire down to Earth, enlivening the growing green world. Taurus is Venus-ruled and symbolized by a bull. Taurus governs the neck, throat chakra, and voice. Like a healthy, earthy garden, Taurus speaks about the joys and work of being in a body and how to create the habits of security and comfort in our daily life.

Challenge: Where you have Taurus in your chart, you can plant your heels and refuse to move. Taurus offers *won't-*power versus willpower; no one can push a bull where it does not want to go. And when you do move, you may have to do so at your own steady pace. Here, also, you can rely too heavily on the material world for contentment, whether that means money, matter, or sensuality. It can lead you to overindulge the senses. Where you have Taurus, you can hoard or hold on, as if possession of that person, place, or thing will solve all. If you look for emotional satisfaction in sexuality or material substance, it will never be enough. If you find yourself too hungry here, ask what you are truly hungry for.

Practical: Taurus loans strength, roots, solidness, reliability, steadiness, and patience. Here you can manage the stuff of this world and bring a common-sense practicality. You can make life a fertile garden, quite literally. Where you have Taurus, you may have magic practically, with growing plants and creatures, as well as figuratively, a place where you can cultivate a creative process, loving relationship, family, or organization. Here, also, you can feed the senses, value beauty and taste, and enjoy being a body.

Gift: Where you have Taurus, your purpose is to breathe life into form. You remind us of all of the grounding power and comfort of our senses. You help us root. The word *matter* comes from *mater*, or *mother*. Taurus witnesses that matter is sacred; matter is the vessel that holds the soul. See that nurturing mother within. Taurus understands loyalty, truly being there for one another. Wherever you have Taurus, you can plant and nurture a garden. This place may take some work but can grow corn for you, giving you a place where you can feed and nurture your community. This Taurus energy can keep the heartbeat for all.

Nurture: If you're feeling stressed, slow down, find your rhythm, and move at your own pace. Notice what your senses tell you, and make yourself fully present to this moment. What do you hear? What do you see? What do you feel under your feet and in your hands? What do you smell and taste? Feed your senses with a touch of grace, good tastes, and wonderful aromas. Notice the heartbeat of the Earth underneath you, grounding you and lending you strength. Feel your roots reach into that Earth and draw that strength up with such abundance that you can send strength to others once again.

GEMINI—CROSS-POLLINATE

The Sun dances through Gemini from May 21 to June 21. Gemini is a mutable air sign, ruled by Mercury, whose symbol is a pair of twins conversing. Gemini is connected to the lungs, shoulders, hands, and nervous system and to siblings and all sibling-like relationships.

Challenge: Gemini encourages breadth, but you have to add the depth. Where you have Gemini, you can gossip, oversimplify, or feel that talking about something is good enough and you won't actually have to do that thing. Your mind can rev like a hamster on a wheel. You can flit from one person to another, one project to another, and never really land. You see the humor but can mistake soundbites and memes for the real story. You may seem like you know more than you do—you do have the words. Because Gemini can charge the nervous system, Gemini energy can point to a place where you get anxious or overthink rather than deeply think. If you are running fast and superficially, or irritating your nerves and becoming anxious, redirect that Gemini flow and give it purpose.

Practical: Gemini points to a part of your life where it pays to network and lead the efforts to communicate. Introduce people who need to know each other, and make your world more interesting. Here you can engage public relations, get the word out, and tune in to the Internet and all the cross-pollinating buzz of communication, which helps you weave the world together. You can find the words and find the humor in any situation. You can pick up language easily and translate from one person to another, from one point of view to another. Here is your way into the town square, where you converse and meet with others and be curious. With that Gemini ability to listen to and understand so many different sources, you can juggle these different voices and help intertwine a diverse population into a team or community.

Gift: Your superpower can be diversifying without being scattered, mobilizing while remaining poised like a spinning top whirling around a calm center. Where you have Gemini, you can be inspired. Take a breath; breathe life into a project. Slow down and add depth to the Gemini brilliance; open your sense of possibility with your mental plethora. Interlace a million ideas—a thousand particles of information—together into a creative whole. In this quarter of your life, if you can communicate—and truly listen—then most any problem can be solved.

Nurture: If you've been overstimulated lately, let your mind wind down and reconnect with your body. Body-centered therapy, a moving meditation like yoga or martial arts, or just dancing in the kitchen can help your brain and body reconnect and reintegrate that escape pod of a busy brain back into wholeness. If, on the other hand, you've been bored to tears lately, engage that busy mind of yours and explore controversial ideas or go down to the coffee shop and share the buzz.

CANCER—IMMERSE

The Sun swims through Cancer from June 22 to July 22. Cancer is the cardinal water sign whose symbol is a crab, an animal that can live in the deep ocean or on the shore and always carries its own protective shell. It is connected to the breasts and stomach and nutrition in and out of the body. Cancer symbolizes your personal home, your homeland, and the oceanic depth of your feelings.

Challenge: Crabs are soft and squishy on the inside and hard with claws and a shell on the outside, an exoskeleton as a means of defense. Where you have the sign of the crab, you can feel immersed in the ocean of emotions. If you are not feeling safe in your heart, those crabby, self-protective defenses can also keep people out, dull the senses, and make it hard to receive warmth and blessings. Conversely, this can be a place where you ask others to take responsibility for you and get stuck in a childlike role, or where you enable others so they stay dependent upon you. Your challenge is to soften defenses and risk believing in your oceanic strength. If you're feeling needy or dependent or find yourself caring for your beloved in a way that enables their bad habits, redirect the Cancer gift and find that nurturing within.

Practical: Where you have Cancer, you have the ability to nurture and cultivate. When your tender core is feeling vulnerable, find someone, or some cause, who needs the help or appreciation more and engage. Here you may find yourself in an echo of family dynamics, so make it a healthy family, the kind you would have loved. Cancer encourages a safe and cozy sanctuary, foods that nurture and comfort, and the ability to apply tough love when needed. It can bring a desire to care for and be cared for by the clan of chosen or biological family. Cancer encourages the role of a cultural parent through social work or community leadership for the good of all. A crab has that protective shell, and healthy Cancer placements support dynamic boundaries, which can make it safer to be vulnerable and alive. Cancer can protect and defend what is valuable to the soul.

Gift: Where you have Cancer, you are asked to dive deep into that sea, down to the oceanic collective consciousness, and come home again. Here you can nourish connections with family and tribe and nourish your body, garden, and community and your temple's hearth. This is a place where you may be able to create a chosen family or step into an emotional leadership position for the good of humankind. A Cancerian planet encourages you to create safety for yourself and others and to act with compassion. With a safe home, in all its metaphoric glory, creativity and affection flow.

Nurture: Take some time in your shell. Even extroverted Cancers or Cancerian planets can feel overwhelmed by other people's emotions, or by adapting to strange new circumstances, and need time within. Find a safe place, whether home or sanctuary, a place that feels familiar and cozy, where you can let your guard down. Connect with old friends, reread a favorite book, or cook comfort foods. As with an old security blanket, spend time with what re-creates safety and comfort for you. Meditate on a healthy relationship to a divine parent and feel held by the collective soul.

LEO—SHINE

The Sun shines in Leo from July 21 to August 22. Leo is the fixed fire sign ruled by the Sun whose symbol is the lion. Leo is connected to the heart, liver, and upper back. Leo energy can be gracious and generous but not necessarily empathic. Where you have Leo, you are asked to be brave and visible and let your light shine for the benefit of all.

Challenge: Wounded Leo energy can find it challenging to walk in another person's shoes. Leo can center itself and forget the needs of others, and say "I am the center of the universe, and you are not." Or you may think troubles are all about you, become paranoid, and choose to avoid people.

Here any attention can feel better than no attention, and this can lead to melodrama or adolescent attention-seeking behavior. If you find yourself craving attention or feeling unhappy with your own company, redirect toward Leo generosity.

Practical: Leo rules the liver and the heart, symbolic of the ability to love and the ability to process the chemistry of emotion. Leo is a fixed sign. Here you can't be bullied or pushed but could be manipulated with approval or attention until you come to love yourself with contentment. You are called to be extroverted, to be aware of the room. Your enthusiasm draws others. You can teach with aplomb, entertain, and sell an idea, object, or skills. Every actor, teacher, leader, or politician needs to activate their Leo energy to hold other people's attention for the collective good. Let this be a place of leadership, talent, and the generosity of your heart.

Gift: Leo encourages you open your heart and express yourself in healthy ways, to take your space within this world. Where you have Leo, you can use your generosity, charm, and warmth to help all feel the joy of life. You can shine your attention on another and make them feel truly seen. Be the hearth fire whose warmth gathers the crowd. Your enthusiasm can authentically uplift and inspire. Share: "I am the center of the universe, and so are you; my heart bows to the divine heart within you."

Nurture: Where you have Leo, you are always aware of interpersonal dynamics, whether you like it or not. To refill your well, investigate what you really need in the moment. Do you need to be completely offstage so you can shut off those antennae that always scan the room and know what other people think and need? Then step into your sanctuary for some "me time" and take care of yourself. If, instead, life has felt boring and has not fed your spark, find the limelight. Find a venue where it's okay to be in the center of the action and you don't have to apologize for shining. Go dancing, show off a skill, share your thoughts in a receptive group. Find another person who needs to be seen, shine the bright beams of your attention on them, and you both benefit.

VIRGO—DIGEST

The Sun works its way through Virgo from August 21 to September 21. The mutable Earth sign Virgo is ruled by Mercury and is symbolized by a woman/Goddess holding a sheaf of wheat, from when wheat was the staff of life. We need to separate the wheat from the chaff, and this ability to differentiate is one of the Virgo gifts. Virgo is connected to the nervous system and intestinal tract, whose job it is to sort nutrient from waste. Wherever you have Virgo, your job is to sort what works from what doesn't, absorb the nutrients of understanding, and steadily improve.

Challenge: You have a very busy mind. Virgo's job is, as we mentioned, to separate the wheat from the chaff, but on a bad day, the Virgo energy holds on to the chaff and loses the grain. Where you have Virgo, you can get stuck on the details and forget they only matter when they are in service of the whole. Virgo rules the guts and nervous system. Here you can physicalize emotions and get sick rather than deal directly with feelings. Here you can get stuck in the paralysis of analysis. You can always see the problem. You can criticize or try to perfect your beloveds as a form of affection, which they may not appreciate. Where you find yourself worrying, fixating on problems, or looking for the weeds and ignoring the flowers, redirect toward Virgo's learning and healing capacities.

Practical: Virgo infuses a healthy work ethic. Virgo loans the ability to analyze, critique, research, understand, and find the words. It helps digest information, to weed and edit. It encourages healing by understanding and repairing systems—physical systems, work systems—and emotional patterns. Bring your deep awareness of the mind-body connection to the job. Weed for the health of the whole garden, and nurture as well as weed. Stay focused on solutions, keep eyes on the long-term goals, and see all the details as steps in that direction.

Gift: Pray rather than worry. Where you have Virgo, you can be deeply empathic and truly understanding. Here you can ask us to really think, rigorously, and not just skim the surface. Virgo can see the humor in the glitches and beauty in the wildflowers and waving grass. Here you can see the potential in a project and people and understand the steps needed to get there. Instead of perfection, seek constant, thoughtful improvement. Here you can be the divine gardener who organizes, weeds, heals, and fertilizes so that the garden grows to its fullest potential.

Nurture: Notice what worries you, concerns you, and irritates you, and what you need to do next. If you need to analyze it, parse it to see the components. Do so in your writing or in a powerful conversation with someone who can analyze with you. Write it down, put all that on your altar, ask your subconscious and back brain to work on it, and then step away. Take a full mental break and either engage your mind in something that will distract you and let your mind reset, like a good movie or book, or take a long shower with good music in the background. Really let go. Absorb something wonderful; use your natural spongelike intuitive ability and soak up great art, meditation, or a walk in the woods.

LIBRA—BALANCE

The Sun walks through Libra from September 22 to October 21. Libra is a cardinal air sign ruled by Venus whose symbol is that of the balancing scales. It is connected to the kidneys, the endocrine system, and all the ways a body comes into balance. Libra calls us to balanced relationship with our soul, a significant other, and a just and fair society.

Challenge: Libra encourages you to see multiple sides of a situation, but that can leave you stuck in the center. Where you have Libra, you may have trouble making decisions or sending clear signals. Here you could perform mental gymnastics to avoid conflict and mistake repression for peace. Here you can get hooked on superficial beauty and forget to look below the surface, or feel lonely, crave romance, and bend yourself out of shape to be what you think others want. If you find yourself addicted to romance and relationship drama, rebalance your life. Be fair to all parties, including you.

Practical: Libra governs the law, justice, equity, mediation, and social justice, and supports true diplomacy. The planets and houses in your chart where you have Libra call in a healthy sense of justice and ask you to be willing to fight fair and negotiate in good faith. You could be outraged if others won't work the same way. Although Libra prefers peaceful negotiations and does not like to get caught in the crossfire, Libra is also the sign of open warfare between equals. Libra calls you to find a healthy work-life mix and invest in healthy relationship dynamics. Here you understand balance in composition and design, and can use beauty in all its forms to affect your world.

Gift: Seeing the inherent beauty in all hearts can be a Libra superpower. Libra's gift is related to the Navajo concept of the Beauty Way, to live in right relations, that is, in balance with all that lives around us, all parts of one's soul, and with Spirit. Where you have Libra, you can see all options and help us know our own hearts better. Know justice; know peace. Here you may be called for random acts of kindness and beauty. Libra can love the otherwise unlovable and just needs to remember that sometimes true love comes as tough love and to model fair, clean, loving boundaries.

Nurture: Step away from contentious situations or any effort to make other people happy and find your own moment of peace. Create a romantic moment with yourself and your muse; spend some time with your art supplies, gardening, cooking, or however you listen to your muse, and create rather than respond to outside stimuli. Invoke beauty, feed your senses, and your wells refill. Contemplate what helps your life feel more in balance with your life purpose. Implement that next step.

SCORPIO—INVESTIGATE

The Sun swims through Scorpio from October 22 to November 21. Scorpio is the fixed water sign ruled by Mars in traditional astrology, co-ruled by Pluto in modern astrology, and is connected to the organs of procreation and elimination, the pelvis, and the root chakra. Scorpio's symbols are both the eagle and the scorpion, the ability to go highest to get perspective, then dive deep to investigate the roots of any matter.

Challenge: Scorpio is nobody's fool, but wherever you have Scorpio, you can overdo it and take suspicion to a fine art. Here you may be drawn to extremes or get deadly serious and wrestle with the deeply primal emotions of jealousy, possessiveness, obsession, and resentment. If you feel unsafe in the compartment of your life where you have Scorpio, you can either withhold and crawl under a rock or sting, or obsess. Here you can obsess over one problem or perpetrator to avoid thinking about other, more complicated issues. Here you may theoretically love all sentient beings but hate the individual in front of you. What you really need is some time alone. In this corner of your life, be careful not to search for confirmation bias, looking only at the information that supports your suspicions. When you feel those primordial extremes, find something wonderful to obsess about.

Practical: Where you have Scorpio, you may be called to do research or be a detective. Concentrate, look deeper, and use your determination and persistence to search, research, be curious, and be fascinated by mystery. Choose carefully where you focus the laser beam of your attention. Scorpio also brings the ability to use humor as a scorpion stinger to defuse a situation or point out some necessary truth—just be aware of the potential consequences. Scorpio rules what is underneath, whether that is in a complex psyche, in the basis of your sexuality, or in the pragmatic deep wells, the basement of your home, plumbing, or foundations. A higher note of Scorpio calls for both a more objective and scientific approach and to look for the true roots of the situation.

Gift: Life is a mystery school. Start your personal investigation here. Scorpio imbues guts and determination. What transforms Scorpio to its higher note is an honest and sincere search for truth. Scorpio asks you to burrow deep, reach into the wellsprings of your soul, your knowledge, and your passion. Look deep beneath the surface, use your intense, laser-like focus and curiosity to search out secrets and solutions. Seek solitude, not isolation, to reconnect with Source. Scorpio may bring you contact with Spirit, spirits, and other dimensions.

Nurture: Take time alone. There is no need to push anybody away, but do find your cave, your study, or your corner of the park that allows you to retreat to an inner temple and listen within. Give yourself time to vent if you need, then let it go. Step away from other people's energies long enough to return to your source, your inspiration. What do you really need here? Look underneath your anger or your strange desires and look for your original hunger, your real need. Honor that as a sacred calling.

SAGITTARIUS—EXPAND

The Sun runs through mutable fire sign Sagittarius from November 22 to December 21. Sagittarius is connected to the thighs, the muscles that propel our movement. Jupiter-ruled Sagittarius's symbol is a centaur, and like that half-human, half-horse creature, Sagittarius points to the human need to travel, roam free, and connect to the natural world.

Challenge: Frank, restless, impatient, and outspoken, Sagittarius energy can be direct to the point of rudeness, cut off from empathy. Where you have Sagittarius, you are encouraged to seek the truth but to not oversimplify nor think your perspective is the only truth. And just because you see it, that doesn't mean you have to say it; timing and pacing are everything. The real shadow of Sagittarius can be to lie to yourself—and so be able to lie to the world—while believing you are honest. Another problem is the shadow side of your ability to see the far horizons, which can mean you miss the problems nearby. Here your need for freedom can be so intense, so afraid you'll be trapped in a bad situation, that you never engage. If you find yourself wandering, unable to commit to person, place, or project, engage that Sagittarian curiosity directly.

Practical: Use your restlessness creatively. Where you have Sagittarius, you are called to go exploring and learn continuously. Expand your world—and therefore be able to expand ours—through education, publishing, broadcast, travel, and the study of philosophy and metaphysics. Healthy, centered Sagittarius energy can make you curious about faraway places and new ideas and encourages you to identify as a global citizen. Travel, hike, camp, and speak for the environment, animals, and children without a voice. Drive, ride, run, and dance. It may be easiest to think about this part of your life when you are moving—walking, driving, or playing with animals.

Gift: Meditate on your personal truth and carry it in your heart. Compassionate truth can be the Sagittarian superpower when your curiosity stays connected to your heart. Wherever you have Sagittarius, you're called to speak the simple and unvarnished reality, without rancor, and often with a sense of humor to make it more palatable. Your curiosity can lead you on a lifetime's journey to open minds and commit to a dynamic future. Like the centaur, Sagittarius mediates between the human and the more-than-human world. Your connection to the natural world can be medicine for both you and those around you.

Nurture: Sagittarius energy needs spaciousness. It needs to feel the barn door is open to relax; instead of walking away from the situation that feels too small, negotiate for more room to breathe. Imagine what it would be like to not run away but expand the situation and the minds involved so it becomes spacious. Go exploring, whether to a strange corner of the town or globe, or explore an idea you hadn't considered before. Envision a life that balances your responsibilities with the freedom to rediscover life on a daily basis. Whether you are watching elephants or romping with a dog, just get outside.

CAPRICORN—ACHIEVE

The Sun works through cardinal Earth sign Capricorn from December 21 to January 20. Capricorn's symbol is a mergoat—half–sea creature, half–mountain goat. It's ruled by Saturn and is connected to our bones and knees, the equipment we use to stand upright, to climb stairs, and to achieve our goals. Wherever you have Capricorn, be prepared to climb.

Challenge: Mountain goats do not walk gracefully on flat terrain. Where you have Capricorn, you need a goal and to feel like you're getting somewhere, step-by-step, or you can get depressed. Capricorn encourages ambition, and here you may be tempted to push others off the mountainside if they're in your way. You can get rigid, righteous, controlling, or judgmental under stress or if you feel someone's pushing or manipulating you. Because honor is so important to Capricorn, if you are not honorable here, expect intense karmic repercussions. If you're frustrated and stuck on the mountainside, redirect that ambition toward the next step.

Practical: No one can climb to the top like a mountain goat. Capricorn encourages healthy ambition and nags you to clarify, define, and achieve a goal with steady steps. Get organized and take personal responsibility. Set a short-term goal that might lead to a long-term goal and accomplish it. Capricorn also wants to build walls, solid foundations, and healthy structures to help you create the future—structures both concrete and metaphorical. Capricorn encourages you to take pragmatic action when you see a problem and know it needs to be fixed.

Gift: Honor, organization, competence, and thoughtful responsibility are Capricornian gifts. Capricorn challenges you to dive deep down into the oceanic collective consciousness, find a worthy dream, then walk it to the mountaintops. Take a dream and bring it into form with kindness, integrity, leadership, and organization. Make your work an offering for all sentient beings.

Nurture: Stop and savor the view. Take a break from the mantle of responsibility. Step away from other people's systems, step out of the chain of command, and neither tell someone what to do nor be told. Create in your mind an

imaginary hall of victories, a room with awards for everything you've ever done right, no matter how small or large,
personal or public, and spend some time in this temple.
With this felt sense of success, go to your oceanic dream
world and imagine where you would love to be in five years,
what vision of the future would make all parts of you happy.
Let that sink in. Notice one small thing that would take you
a notch closer, then step forward.

AQUARIUS—COLLABORATE

The Sun sits in the fixed air sign Aquarius from approximately January 20 to February 18. Aquarius is ruled by Saturn in traditional astrology, co-ruled by Uranus in modern
astrology, and is connected to the ankles, which we use
to turn from one direction to another when walking in a
crowd. The symbol for Aquarius is the water bearer—not the
water itself, but the person fetching, carrying, and pouring
the water, a great service to the community.

Challenge: Where you have Aquarius in your chart,
you can get spacey, lost, or disconnected. Here you may be
tempted to talk yourself out of honest emotions because
of some philosophical rebellion or because you are overly
aware of what others might think and get stuck in what you
think you "should" feel. Because you're naturally farsighted,
you may need a pair of emotional reading glasses; you can
see the big picture but miss the feelings of the people next
to you. Here your challenge is to know what you feel at the
same time you reach out and build intimacy with others.
Where you feel that emotional disconnect, ask what you're
avoiding; redirect that Aquarian vision to see the whole picture, near and far.

Practical: Here you are called to collaborate, to both honor
the collective experience and revere the communication it

takes to create this healthy collaboration. Where you have Aquarius, you have the key ability to understand how the group works, what's expected, what others need, and how best to work in a team. You can help us see beyond our individual needs and see the bigger picture. If you start from an honest perception of what's going on, even if it goes ágainst your original theory, you can develop new philosophies or policies that help us work together.

Gift: Aquarius holds a paradox, which, when well balanced, becomes a multidimensional gift. Aquarius's traditional ruler Saturn asks you to know what society expects. Aquarius's co-ruler Uranus encourages you step outside of the box and reinvent the form. Together, these two poles create tension, but that tension can help you find an authentic and original path through the center. Aquarius offers a natural political knack, an awareness of what your family, tribe, or community needs, and an abstract, iconoclastic soul.

Nurture: Get perspective and see the bigger picture. Step away from the complexities of intimate personal relationships and get some fresh air. Consider watching or participating in a team sport. Enjoy live music and other shared ecstatic experiences. Meditate with a group. Work together with like minds on a cause that calls your heart. Contemplate your philosophical framework: Are you being true to your path, or does your philosophy need to adapt to the reality you see?

PISCES—SENSITIZE

The Sun drifts through mutable water sign Pisces from February 19 to March 20. Pisces is ruled by expansive Jupiter in traditional astrology and intuitive Neptune in modern astrology and is associated with the feet. Where you have Pisces, you are sensitive, may feel squishy and vulnerable, can empathize with ambient emotions, and are easily moved to compassionate action.

Challenge: Sensitivity. Wherever you have Pisces, you may feel unusually permeable, overly sensitive to pain and prickles, or wishy-washy. Be wary of either a disempowering victim mentality or a fierce flashback to pain. In this corner of your life, you can absorb energy and thoughts from your surroundings. You can get confused about what are your feelings and what are another's, easily overwhelmed by what you pick up. Here, also, you can be charming, so charming that truth becomes ephemeral. You may long to escape from nitty-gritty reality, either into difficult substances or a world of your own imaginings. If you get an intuitive hit and don't have the facts, you can invent a story to explain the feelings and head way off base. Be aware of that fine line between intuition and imagination.

Practical: Here you can use your subtlety and perception in pragmatic ways, so make it safe to be sensitive. Tune in to artistic sensitivities, healing sensitivities, and your compassionate nature. Make sure you are as sensitive to your own needs as you are of others, and as perceptive of their sensitivities as you are of your own. Bring these subtle perceptions into whatever work you do, whether you work with cars, kids, or as a detective, with essential oils or as a counselor.

Gift: Your imagination is a rich and bubbling wellspring, so tap into it. You perceive the human psychic permeability; like the fertile swamps and wetlands where the Piscean fish live, you are aware of the interconnectedness of your ecosystem, in all its metaphors. Your courage is supple, like a river reed that bends in the currents. Sensitivity, perception, intuition, imagination, and kind generosity can be your superpowers. You may be aware of Spirit, ambience, the vibes of a place. You can teach others to seek, honor, and eventually understand dreams and visions.

Nurture: Make it safe and wonderful to be sensitive. Take some time out of ordinary reality and step into imagination, disappear into a good book or wander through a flowering field. Feed the sensitivities with lovely sights, wonderful smells, and music that brings joy. Spend time sharing deeper feelings and subtle sensitivities with kindred souls. Use those extraordinary senses. Study basic psychic protection and grow more comfortable with this skill. Meditate and become permeable to the universal Spirit so that you may return refreshed and inspired.

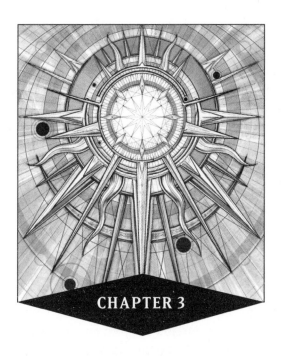

CHAPTER 3

YOUR INNER POPULATION: LUMINARIES, ASTEROIDS, AND LUNAR NODES

THE SUN, MOON, AND ASCENDANT

If you meet another astro-interested person, they'll ask you what your Sun, Moon, and ascendant, or rising, signs are. These three points form the frame upon which the rest of the chart is built. The Sun speaks of your basic nature, the Moon of your inner emotional patterns, and the ascendant describes how you interface with the world. Like sketching out the face and getting the eyes, nose, and mouth in the right place and the proportions first, these points are foreground; all the details fill out from there. There are 1,728 variations of this triumvirate, so just this skeleton gives you a lot of information to work with.

We will cover the ascendant in Chapter 5, as it is the cusp of the first house. For now just think of it as your front door, the entrance into your chart.

LUMINARIES: YOUR SHINING LIGHTS

Sun: Source—Your life force. All the other planets reflect its light.

Moon: Perception—Your inner world, your emotional prime directive.

From the Earth, the Sun and Moon, our symbols of consciousness and unconscious, appear to be the same size in the sky or we couldn't have an eclipse, an interesting coincidence of relative size and distance. We are probably the only planet with this view. From our symbolic astrological perspective, the Moon is as important as the Sun.

In the next chapter, we'll cover the rising sign, the front door to your chart, and all the house placements. Here we'll focus on the energetic core of the chart, the Sun and Moon, and then go through the planets as they reflect that Sun's light.

You have a team of planets, a whole family of them in your chart, and as with any team, it can be difficult if everybody's a leader. Your dignified planets, those in their strongest placement, will express more easily and more true to type. If this were a football team, you'd throw them the ball because they are well supported and have an open field.

Your planets with a more complex placement, not so true to type, like macho Mars in Venus-ruled Libra, call you to be self-aware and conscious, and encourage you to find your own way through to the subtlety and understanding that can make you unique. You can think of these planets as the Bohemians: the artists and inventors, the self-employed, those who find their own path and encourage you to do the same. We'll go over these qualities with each planet.

Dignified: Every planet and luminary can feel strongest in the sign it rules, called its rulership, or domicile, and a sign that fits its disposition easily, where it is exalted. The traditional planets are either diurnal or nocturnal; they have a time of day they are happiest or strongest, and here they are called *in sect.*

Debilitated: A planet in the sign opposite to its rulership is in detriment, out of its element, and thus has to get creative about its expression. A planet in the sign opposite its exalted state is in its fall. Each traditional planet has a time of day when they are less comfortable and less strong, or out of sect. Those planets work with less ease, and they operate with more complexity and invention.

THE SUN—SOURCE

When you feel overwhelmed, tired, or have trouble making your place in the world, talk to your Sun. Maybe you feel the spotlight has been too bright, and you're exhausted. Meditation with the Sun can encourage you to take your place at the center to feel energized and help you shine for the benefit of all.

When someone asks you what sign you are, they're asking what sign the Sun shone through the day you were born. The Sun symbolizes your connection to Source, the point where life force flows into your life and your chart. It is our star. All the rest of the planets reflect the Sun's light, so while the Sun's sign does not define you, it does set the tone for the chart.

Notice the sign of your Sun, the time of day you were born, whether your Sun is exalted, debilitated, or somewhere in between. This doesn't define who you are, but it sets the lighting tone for the rest of the chart. Think about this for a minute, and journal how your life reflects your Sun's sign and how it does not.

The sign the Sun shines through at your birth, and the house it inhabits, describes your source of basic vitality, the core of your personality. The Sun spends a month in each sign and circles through the zodiac once a year. It rules Leo, it is exalted in Aries, and it is stronger in a daytime chart. Here the personality shines easily. The Sun's expression is more complex, more subtle, and possibly more in need of support in a nighttime chart and in Aquarius (opposite Leo) and Libra (opposite Aries), signs where the person can feel more aware of others than themselves.

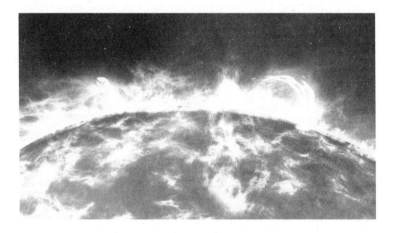

To look at the Sun directly can blind you, but if you look at its magnificence through a carefully filtered telescope, you can see a little bitty peach fuzz on the surface of its giant curve. That peach fuzz is about one Earth thick. The Sun is unimaginably huge.

Challenge: When your Sun is exaggerated, you might want to take up all the oxygen in the room and could forget to respect the shining light in each soul you meet. You could use personal charm or a powerful personality to manipulate for your own ends, oblivious to other points of view. You could have difficulty integrating your needs with those around you until you choose to respect the Sun within all others. Whereas an under-energized Sun—debilitated or in stressful aspects to difficult planets—can leave you feeling easily tired, as if you are not living in line with your Source. Tough aspects to the Sun can point to how your self-respect and identity might have been dented as a child and left you vulnerable to attack. To help heal any of these extremes, develop your Sun's gift and learn to express it directly.

Practical: The sign, house, and aspects of your Sun describe how the universal energy enters your life and flows through you. A healthy Sun brings a healthy, sturdy, resilient ego. Your personality shines through the Sun's sign, with all its pros and cons. It is the point where energy comes into your chart and life, the stage upon which you can shine, and it offers clues to build your health, vitality, and strength.

Gift: The Sun describes your source of warmth, the light that shines from within you and illuminates your personal hearth fire. It symbolizes what excites you or charges you up, how you feel about yourself, and the nature and characteristics of the light you shine. As you let the Sun's life force flow through you and do whatever you do well and with joy, your health can improve. You draw support toward you. Step into your potential. When you center yourself in a healthy way and shed the projections of others upon you, you can gain a generous strength.

Affirmation: I am one with the center of the universe, and so are you. I matter, and so do you. I am connected to Source.

Solar Activity: The Chart's Volume Control

The Sun is the power source for our solar system and our charts. All the planets reflect its glorious light. The surface of the Sun is always roiling as this huge energy generator pulses, and its pulses act like the volume control for all the other planets and aspects of astrology. When the Sun is in its active cycle, solar flares—eruptions of electromagnetic radiation—shoot out in coronal mass ejections many times the size of Earth, which infuse charged particles throughout the solar system. Then the Sun quiets down. While it still burns intensely, it does so without those dark, roiling sunspots or shooting solar flares.

The Sun activates and quiets on a roughly 11-year cycle, but it does not conform to a predictable schedule, to the frustration of both astrologers and astronomers. While the cycle usually varies between 9 to 13 years, the Sun was unusually quiet for decades during the height of the baroque period in the second half of the 17th century. The Sun was unusually active during the American Revolution, the French Revolution, and the mid-1960s. You can look up on the Internet the Sun's activity around the month of your birth. See SpaceWeather.com for the solar activity of this moment. Neither solar extreme is better than the other—we need both perspectives. The solar level does not change the nature of the chart, but it does turn the volume up or down.

Solar Flares: Activate

Change is in the air. When the Sun is active, our upper atmosphere absorbs its charged particles and we experience beautiful aurora borealis here on Earth. Our atmosphere vibrates with these charged particles, and we can experience interruptions in our electrical systems. These active solar cycles correspond with an increased activity in politics and the restless search for new answers. It turns up the volume on all the other astrological aspects. Those born in an active solar cycle tend to stay involved in the world, aware of action here on Earth. To an already practical chart it can make them anywhere from highly political or practically efficient, to Earth bound and aggressive. To a spiritual or inspirational chart, it adds a practical, world/action, political perspective and can increase the vitality.

Solar Calm: Clarify

When the Sun quiets down, the crops quiet down, the solar static lessens, and we can see farther into space. It can be hard to motivate political change during a solar minimum. People seem to accept their situation, even if they grumble about it. People seem less likely to search for new answers, but momentum can still build in the direction the culture is already headed. The cultural world tends to grow richer as our minds turn more to the arts and spiritual or religious questions. We can see and hear deeper into space when the Sun is quieter.

People born during solar minimums tend to have more porous immune systems and can be more interested in theory or understanding than action, and more interested in the abstract or the artistic and in life beyond the bright light of action here on Earth, for better or worse. To a practical chart, a quiet Sun adds a more ephemeral touch, encourages a more universal perspective, or puts religion or philosophy on the front burner. Many astrologers, artists, and occultists are born under a solar minimum. To an already-ephemeral chart, a quiet Sun can send them floating into the ozone, making it a challenge to stay involved and active here on Earth. To a politically oriented person, it can correlate with less interest in observing what the people need and more focus on applying their theory or philosophy. We can choose to balance the solar flow with our awareness and an effort to balance our worldview. We *always* have choice.

THE MOON: PERCEPTION

If you feel out of touch with your emotions or swamped by them or need comfort and want to feel more at home in the world, spend time with your Moon. Wake up this archetype of acceptance and loving care; walk with a universal Kind Mother energy.

The Sun is unimaginably huge—the Earth's Moon is relatively small—but through that miraculous balance of distance and proportion, the Sun and Moon appear to be the same size—half a degree of arc—or we wouldn't see an exact eclipse. The Moon is our inner source of light.

The Moon takes two and a half days in each sign and describes what moves you. It symbolizes the inner rivers of your emotions, what motivates you, how you express your feelings, and how you nurture and need nurturance. Because that inner river runs so deep, it often runs below our conscious awareness, and so those feelings and habits can surprise even us. The trick with the Moon is to become conscious of that inner motivating river, to know those emotional patterns—your needs, moods, and habits—trained by your childhood and that can affect you throughout the rest of your life.

Think of this layering of Sun and Moon like cutting into a blood orange. This fruit may look like an orange on the outside, but within you find rich, red pulp. If you dissect someone born with the Sun in Aries and Moon in Cancer, they may structure their life like a brave, independent, impulsive Aries but feel like a sensitive, thoughtful, self-protective Cancer Moon who could use some reassurance on the inside.

Meditate with your Moon sign and think about how this might describe your inner world, your emotional patterns. Notice from which house its energy radiates into your chart. That place describes your soul-source, what brings you comfort and what calls you to your deepest interpersonal work.

The Moon is most Moon-like, nurturing and emotionally alive, in a nighttime chart, in the sign it rules, Cancer, or in Taurus, where it is exalted because it grounds and stabilizes. The Moon is less comfortable in a daytime chart and in the signs Capricorn (opposite Cancer), where it can feel paradoxically nurtured through work, and Scorpio (opposite Taurus), where it taps into primal depths.

Challenge: The Moon speaks of a primary emotional need that you bring into this life and through which the universe seems to trick you into your toughest work. If you find yourself pouting, jealous, sullen, or vengeful, and you're not quite sure why, check to see what tweaked your Moon. Your Moon doesn't describe your logical nature; it describes those underground rivers of feelings, which run under your consciousness, often right through your blind spots. It points to a place where you can feel needy, insecure, dependent, and subjective. It records early family patterning and all its unconscious material. A wounded Moon can either bring overwhelming irrational emotions or a fierce need for nurturance and safety; conversely, it can also give you trouble connecting to your feelings and motivation. If you are feeling needy or estranged from your feelings, or surprised by the strength of some primal emotion, get to know your Moon and learn how to bring it comfort.

Practical: Other parts of your chart will tell you what you want to do with your life; the sign and house of the

Moon tell you how you want to do it and where you want to go home at the end of the day. If you want to make someone feel at home, look to the sign of their Moon. The Moon embodies how you perceived your mother and maternal influences—or your primary nurturers—as a child. It sketches out how you need to be nurtured now and how you tend to nurture others. The Moon talks about how you deal with the public and how you host your guests. It signifies your daily habits, how you cook, and how you train your dog, all the little things you can take for granted in your life.

Gift: When you cooperate with your Moon's prime directive and needs, you'll find it easier to walk your path and walk it in harmony. You are one with the ebb and the flow. Here is your sanctuary; here you communicate with the Divine Parent within. Here you can understand and take responsibility for your emotional needs. Be the hands of the Divine Parents here on Earth and feed, support, encourage, nurture, and set healthy boundaries with the people around you.

Affirmation: My inner world is valid. I have a right to my feelings, my dreams, and what helps me feel at home.

Moon Phases

The relationship between the Sun and Moon defines the Moon phases. A chart cannot tell you whether someone is an old soul or young one, but it can point out if you are on a learning curve of a particular karmic cycle or in the resolution phase. We all have so many karmic cycles to go through on our soul's journey, so this is not a place to judge or compare progress. When the Moon is waxing, the soul is gaining experience on this particular karmic cycle, exploring and confronting new patterns and information. When the Moon waning, past the full Moon point and heading toward the new Moon, it is integrating and resolving knowledge and patterns both from their karmic past and within the family lineage.

THE MOON THROUGH THE SIGNS

If you were born under an **Aries Moon**, you can love deeply but still need to prioritize your own inner calling; listen to your muse first and others second. Learn to include both wherever possible. Direct, intense, generous, and fiercely independent, you love a challenge and buck authority but are gold in an emergency. You hate being told what to do, even if you were about to do it, and so are good at guiding and leading others without disempowering them. It's more comfortable for you to work in fits and bursts than a steady effort, to work on projects rather than on the same thing every day. Your challenge will be to learn patience with people who work at a different speed than you. The parenting you received may have been erratic, which made it easier to just do it yourself—and do it your way. It is still easier for you to do something yourself than coordinate, but this can limit your efforts until you can envision dynamic collaboration with other independent souls. Spontaneity revives you. You can either irritate or inspire others with your innate fire; it's your choice. You might tend to cook fast, burn food, and be surprised that your dog or children don't get what you're teaching. Your energy is bountiful and direct when your actions align with your inner calling.

If you were born under a **Taurus Moon**, underneath it all you seek stability and security by your definition. You know the sacredness of the senses and of steady living in right relations with the world around you. The Taurus Moon loans you the stubbornness and stability of an oak tree: solid, strong, stable, sensual, glorious, with resources to share. You prefer to work at your own pace, dislike being rushed, and tend to opt for the secure garden rather than the unknown potential. While you may love your own traditions and are comforted by daily habits and good food, you can accept that other people need to do things differently. You could be a wonderful cook or a great host for a conference. While you are open-minded, you cannot be moved once you dig in your heels. Stability was probably considered precious by the people around you when you were growing up. But prisons are stable; make sure to be specific about what you want to last. Be willing to leave dysfunction and find a healthy place to take root. Your challenge is to explore the difference between strength and stubbornness and to learn flexibility when it's time to reach past familiarity and through the unknown for a more fertile life.

If you were born under a **Gemini Moon**, you can talk to anybody, anywhere, when you want to. Your rhythm is innately versatile. When you were young, you may have had to adapt to different households or differing personalities and learned how to mutate to fit your changing circumstance. You can translate ideas, cultures, and opinions, and can get along with people no one else understands. However, you might sometimes feel self-conscious about your words. Multitasking can be easy for you. You can get bored, and when you get bored, you can make mistakes. If those mistakes or small accidents proliferate, find a way to reengage your whole attention to where you are at that moment. Sometimes you may need to hide in the Internet, video games, a good book, or anything that uses that rapid-fire brain and doesn't demand a lot of you emotionally. You're a natural extrovert and people person yet can get anxious when overextended and need time alone to retract your antennae and reconnect to your Source. You are challenged to keep your busy nervous system connected to your heart, to look for answers that are deep as well as broad, and to find the value in stillness.

If you were born under a **Cancer Moon**, you search for what nurtures body, soul, and culture. The Cancer Moon imbues natural empathy and sensitivity. Tender awareness can be your superpower, though you can throw on your armor when you're feeling vulnerable. You can help others feel safe and so fulfill their potential. You nurture family, chosen family, students, patients, homes, and businesses. Your creativity arises from your introspection. You can swim around in that deep inner ocean. You can feel the needs of the people around you; you hurt when they hurt, which can make you aggravated with them if they're not taking care of themselves. If you are feeling overwhelmed by people, solitude, safety, and time in your shell will refill the wells. Your challenge is to nurture yourself as much as others; parent yourself the way you would like to have been parented, not necessarily the way you were; and to step beyond your defenses, finding strength in your spine and not just the protection of your shell.

If you were born under a **Leo Moon**, you can warm the room like a hearth fire and be an inspiring cultural or social center post, if you so choose. You can add panache to any circumstance and draw people's attention to you for their benefit, as a teacher, host, performer, or one who inspires. When you were young you may have felt at the very center, for better or worse, or felt emotionally responsible for some adult around you who should have been responsible for their own story. You are so aware and emotionally tuned in to your audience that occasionally your antennae feel burned out and you need time offstage or with just a few loving people. With your warmth and generosity, people can miss your quiet and deep stubbornness. Leo is a fixed sign. You might so crave an interesting and dramatic life that you create emergencies; you would rather see the house burned down than be bored. Your challenge will be to not hide in melodrama, but to express directly and with integrity, share the spotlight, and see beauty in your daily surroundings.

If you were born under a Virgo Moon, you came here to learn, diagnose, and heal. You consider your work on yourself or your craft an ongoing project and engage in constant thoughtful improvement but may have trouble telling when something is good enough or even have confidence that you are good enough. Your family may have fed you a running critical or improving commentary that sharpened your skills but built in your psyche a pervasive, whispering inner critic and editor. As you are always aware of what needs improvement, you can be a great social critic, editor, or teacher but can be hard on yourself and don't really need or want critical comments from others. Your challenge is to weed in order to nurture a beautiful garden, to see potential in all the flowers and fruits. You may also feel unusually connected to ancient wisdom teachings and traditional healing methods. If you develop self-forgiveness and playfulness along the way, you can guide us to heal and grow with intelligence and compassion.

If you were born under a **Libra Moon**, you can be a natural mediator, blessed with kindness and diplomacy. You may have felt the need to be a peacemaker between family members as a child or have been put in that situation. You can usually see both sides of an argument, and while you can take the lead in a healthy fight for a good cause, you may get anxious around more personal confrontation, particularly hating being caught between warring friends. You might be described as a people pleaser but are naturally gracious and work to keep peace. Relationships of all types are where you learn and shine. Beauty and proportion soothe you; your surroundings affect you. Your challenge is to learn how to handle conflict directly, decide quickly, and not enable others in the process. Learn to contribute to everyone's happiness without taking responsibility for their emotional conditions; you cannot do their work for them. Lead us toward dynamic cooperation and peaceful coexistence.

If you were born under a **Scorpio Moon**, you love a mystery and have guts and determination. You also have the capacity for a laser-like focus or an obsessive streak, so you need to choose carefully where you concentrate your attention. You may have an active subconscious and can tap deeply into primal emotions. Early in your life, you could have felt alone;possibly your parents were distracted by their own story in your early years. You will always need moments of solitude to unwind and tap into your deep well of inspiration, but you do not need to isolate. While you can be deeply stubborn, one way to get your cooperation is to engage your curiosity. You love to investigate; you want to turn every stone over and can be naturally suspicious. Small, invasive details can upset you, but you are good when the chips are down; you can confront challenges that make others quake. Your challenge is to be flexible, kind, and curious rather than judgmental. Become a guide into the mysteries of your chosen field.

If you were born under a **Sagittarius Moon**, you can be naturally playful, exploratory, restless, and upbeat. If you are given lemons, you make lemonade. You can be radically and unpolitically honest, like the mythic child who told the emperor he had no clothes when everyone else pretended he was dressed splendidly. People tend to believe you because you can speak the truth uncharged and with acceptance. But you can also make up a scenario and believe your own story. Remember to question, rather than assume, your truths. Talking about complex emotions can make you nervous. It can be easier for you to do so if you are walking, driving, or moving. You hate to feel trapped and prefer to drive yourself to the party so you can leave when you're ready. You may decorate with mementos from your travels or from where you would like to travel. Your taste in food is eclectic and quick—either world foods or fast food. You are challenged to learn tact, to ask good questions, look deeper, and solve problems rather than change the subject or move away. When your heart is open, you understand our connection to all beings around the globe.

If you were born under a **Capricorn Moon**, you came here with a job to do. You may have come into a family who defined themselves by what they did rather than who they are. Rarely did an adult look at you and ask you how you felt. Possibly love was shown by doing something for you, working harder, cooking, fixing, or controlling, rather than being emotionally present to you. You may define yourself by your competence, feel loved when your work is appreciated, and may need to learn a broader self-acceptance to blossom. When you can offer yourself and others that encouragement, you can lead, coordinate teams, and build blueprints. You have uncommonly good common sense. You can keep your emotions under control, which can make you look cool, calm, and collected under stress; you could be the most levelheaded person in a real crisis. But if you need a hug, you may have to ask for it directly, because no one will notice. Your challenge is to accept you are worthy even when you're sitting still, and to appreciate the more subtle or diverse worth of other, less organized souls.

If you were born under an **Aquarius Moon**, you came to tend the interconnected will-web of community. You could either be eccentric or know all the rules too well, blending in with the social norms or enjoying redefining all the goals; in any scenario, whether you blend in, rebel, or re-create, you are keenly aware of the group zeitgeist. When you were young, your family may have been unusually aware of what the larger family or community thought. You are emotionally farsighted, aware of far horizons and so can build teams and help people work together but may have a harder time sensing the needs of the people nearest you, unless you choose to look. You have a philosophical bent to your soul, but make sure your philosophy is grounded in real experience. You can get abstract about your emotions, so your challenge is to stay in touch with your true feelings, not what you think you should feel, and to see intimate beloveds as clearly as you see the bigger picture.

If you were born under a **Pisces Moon**, you feel everything. Other people may talk about empathy, but you honestly feel all the feels, particularly emotional sensations that other people aren't willing to admit they are experiencing. When you were young, a parent may have been uncomfortable with their own emotions or suppressed them, but you felt them anyway. That sensitivity can physicalize. You have allergies or environmental sensitivities that make no sense to others but also can feel healed by subtle energy medicine and thoughtful changes. You are guided by your intuition. You notice things that others miss. You get the problem, bring a creative viewpoint to most every situation, and are capable of profoundly compassionate action. You may be unusually open to ghosts, spirits, and the environmental atmosphere, so study basic psychic protection to become comfortable with this skill. While you can get your feelings hurt easily and can get edgy if cornered or guilt-tripped, you are deeply supportive when you feel safe. Your challenge is to make it safe to be sensitive, to become more comfortable with ordinary reality. When you can trust your flexible, willowy strength, you encourage awareness, vision, and imagination in those around you.

ASTEROIDS

The personality of the asteroids add richness and depth to your chart, but remember their relative importance; just as you might sketch the proportions of a face first and then add the mole, the scar, the line of the eyebrow, always start with the framework of the chart—the planets, houses, and aspects—before adding in asteroids and other subtle points. These five asteroids are most used in astrology, but there is a whole band of them between Mars and Jupiter and a few more scattered elsewhere throughout the solar system.

Chiron: Heal

Chiron is minor planet or planetoid between Saturn and Uranus and acts as a bridge between the traditional planets (visible to the naked eye) Sun through Saturn and the outer planets of Uranus and beyond (those only be seen by telescope). Chiron symbolizes what you learned in the school of hard knocks and how you can use that knowledge to help others. It describes the training you receive from solving problems and healing your wounds. Even if you never quite heal in this place of karmic tenderness, you'll have wisdom to pass on—once you metabolize that experience, that is.

Challenge: Chiron points to a place where you can be easily provoked, where you might have touchy memories or full-on PTSD, a place where you may always need to be aware of your triggers and be very gentle with yourself.

Practical: Chiron symbolizes what you learned that other people need to know. Take the training, practice what you learn, and teach it when you feel the call.

Gift: Compost the pain and troubles of the past and they become fodder for wise compassion. Think back through your life and notice some of the tough or touchy events you experienced here, by sign and house. We cannot say why you went through those experiences, but you can choose to use those as cosmic-training-developed wisdom, compassion, and tools to help others.

Note the house and sign of your Chiron and scan back through your memories. What test, challenge, or wounding event did you experience that is related to this area? What did you learn from it? What strength did you build, and how has this helped you help others?

Ceres: Nurture

Ceres is the largest element in the asteroid belt between Mars and Jupiter, named after the Roman goddess of harvest and earthly fertility who wrangled with Pluto over her daughter Proserpina. Ceres in your chart points to the complex dynamics around mothering and being mothered, how you experienced that parent-child dynamic—for better or worse—and how that dynamic works for you as an adult. Ceres also intimates a potential place of profound rebirth; once the Greek version, Demeter, completed her task as parent, she started an ancient mystery school, which derived their secret from metaphors of the harvest: cut the heads off grain with the scythe, bury them, and through this, new life arises.

Challenge: A problematic Ceres can point to potential digestive issues or eating disorders. If you felt controlled by others' power over your daily needs, you may crave to be in control of your body now. Choose to do it in a nurturing way. A troubled Ceres can point to custody issues and tension around parenting and being parented.

Practical: *Ceres* is the root word for *cereal* and has to do with what feeds your body and your soul: agriculture, nutrition, digestion, care, and even a good spa day. The house where

Ceres resides can also point to a compartment of your life where you may need to stand up and protect the vulnerable.

Gift: Ceres asks you to be open to being mothered by Spirit. Here you can reach toward the Great Mother, the archetype of all parenting, when you need to channel nurturance to yourself or others. Ceres also points to your soul work once your family years are complete, whether it is a child, career, or project you raised. She also encourages you to see your post-nurturing years as an adventurous mystery school.

Note the house and sign of your Ceres and scan back through your memories. How were you mothered? How would you like to have been mothered instead? What was your training around food, nurturance, and caretaking? How can you better nurture yourself and therefore have more to share with others?

Pallas Athena: Think

Pallas signifies placing your chart where you may channel a certain kind of sharp intelligence that may or may not be connected to your heart. That connection is something you need to consciously maintain. Pallas Athena speaks of your ability to manifest and craft what your imagination can produce. The Goddess Athena was birthed fully armed out of her father Zeus's forehead after he swallowed her mother when his jealous wife came around—a story that symbolizes guarded intellect that doesn't easily acknowledge its emotional origins.

Challenge: Pallas points to where you can get stuck in your mental defenses, where you rationalize and duel with your wits, where you may not always be able to drop into your heart and speak from compassion. In the house where she resides, you could be tempted to deny your mother and your receptive nature, whatever gender you are, and lead with your sharp edges. Given the chance to either be right or be happy, Pallas Athena points to where you might want to be right.

Practical: This asteroid speaks of a place in your chart where you can build your craft through weaving, sculpting, negotiating, and through pursuits of the mind, academic and logical.

Gift: Athena can call you to develop your leadership in the house where she resides and in response to the planets she aspects. She brings the empowered thinking, leadership, fierce intelligence that can work for the good of all. She calls you to step up and live up to your potential.

Note the house and sign of your Pallas Athena and muse about how you balance your mind and heart. What is the nature of your mental defenses? How do you best learn? What helps you integrate your thoughts and your feelings? How does this Pallas Athena call you into leadership, and how do you feel about that role?

Juno: Partnership

Juno can give you hints about what you need to feel secure in real partnership and where you might believe you have to choose between a healthy egalitarian relationship and work you loved. Juno calls you to create healthy compromise between equals while moving forward in line with your life purpose. Mythic Juno was the daughter of Saturn, wife of Jupiter, mother of Mars, and queen organizer of society. She had to redefine her work, often fight for it, once she mated with Jupiter, but together they modeled an uneasy but equal partnership that took a lot of work and had great rewards.

Challenge: Juno asks you to look at your training around relationships and question any assumptions about partnership rooted deep in your childhood. Where Juno resides in your chart can point out where you might either avoid relationships for the sake of work or lean too far in relationships and either give up your path or try to live out your ambitions through your partner. Juno points to how jealousy and possessiveness can get triggered when you're out of balance.

Practical: Juno teaches relationship skills and all the complexity that entails. In any relationship, not just marriage, the position and aspects to Juno can offer resources to mediate between you and a beloved and help you hold your own while you learn healthy relationship skills. Juno asks you to get in there and do the work needed for long-term connections of all kinds.

Gift: Any loving relationship can act as a spiritual path. The deeper the love and the commitment, the more it calls you into a spiritual cauldron of transformation. Juno calls you to step out of your assumptions and training, hold your own, do your work, take care of yourself, and open to the alchemical work of relationships.

Note the house and sign of your Juno and ponder your models for relationships. Were you encouraged to believe you could balance your career or calling and a healthy, egalitarian relationship? Look within and think about any belief systems that might stand in the way of partnerships. What would it look like if you could be both fully realized in your life and in mutually supporting relationships, and what can you do now to step closer to that?

Vesta: Hearth

The house where Vesta resides points to your inner hearth fire, a spiritual home within, and a place where your inner light can be fed and warm the lives of others. The second-largest asteroid between Jupiter and Mars is named after Vesta, ancient goddess of hearth and home, the center of a strong community. The fire in her temple was never allowed to go out, and the fire in the heart of every home is sacred to her.

Challenge: Vesta can point out where in your chart and how you tend to overextend yourself or enable others. The house where she exists can be a part of your life where you get caught up in other people's circus and lose your center, burn yourself up to help others, and then have nothing left to give. Conversely, with too little expression, here you can feel isolated and alone if you forget to share your warmth.

Practical: Vesta points to where you can take refuge, how you can step away from a too-loud world, from partisan politics, and renew. Here you can build a temple.

Gift: Where Vesta sits in your chart you are called to stay true to yourself, centered in your own heart. She invites you to become comfortable with your own company, a place where you are connected to Spirit. She helps you find that inner flame that loans you strength and connects you to your wisdom. Here you learn that the healthiest, strongest boundaries help you have more to give, to be a hearth fire for yourself and others.

Note the house and sign of your Vesta and look within. What renews you, brings you back to center, and allows you to hear yourself and to hear Spirit? What does your inner temple look like? How does time within, time in self-care, help prepare you to engage the world more fully?

THE LUNAR NODES: KARMIC DIRECTION

The nodes offer a personal compass, a clear map for our souls' growth this lifetime. The north and south lunar nodes are the points on the zodiac where the Moon's orbit crosses the ecliptic. These points are always directly opposite one another and can be read as a unit, a progression from south node to north node. These points were traditionally called the head and the tail of the dragon because it appeared as if some huge being draped itself across the sky. When the Moon, Sun, and Earth exactly line up, Earth experiences an eclipse, as if the Sun or Moon is covered by the shadow of that great dragon.

Read the south nodes as a continuum. We work from the south node toward the north node in our lifetime, bunny-hopping back and forth between them, but with an evolutionary direction. They work as a pair. Look to the nodes for direction. Look to the sign and house of the south node for practical skills that can take you toward the house and sign of the north node.

South Node—Past

North Node—Future

Challenge: The dragon's tail, where the Moon descends south and crosses over the Sun's path, symbolizes what skills, gifts, weaknesses, and karmic problems you brought in from other lives. It speaks of unfinished business for you to work on and skills you were born with and need to apply now.

We often look for an answer in the south node, as it is charged with subliminal memories from other lives, but that direction will never quite scratch our itch. The south node holds karmic memories, often connected to the body part ruled by the sign and house of that node, a part that needs extra TLC and attention. It can point to a problem that looks like such a simple thing to fix from the outside but is deeply complicated on the inside and needs patience. Don't get stuck in your south node, but do honor the depths of the work it represents.

Practical: The south node speaks of what we walked in with, and the north node calls us to head in that direction. We need to use the skills we bring in from the south toward this unexplored but intriguing territory.

Gift: Where the Moon heads north over the ecliptic is called the north or ascending node and was seen as the dragon's head. The north node has answers. It symbolizes new material for you this lifetime, a place you need to explore, develop, and evolve. It has no charge from past lives or early experience, so it can seem boring until you begin to develop it. The north node is a point toward which you may long, toward which to grow, a place that brings you joy as you develop it, a place that can bring comfort and satisfaction as you grow older.

Look at the sign and house of your nodes and think about the direction of evolution in your life. What skills and talents and what unfinished business or difficulties do you recognize around your south node? What skills or new material are you being called to develop over time related to your north node?

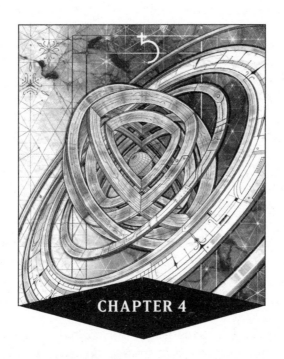

CHAPTER 4

WANDERING CELESTIAL CHARACTERS: THE PLANETS

The word *planet* derives from the ancient Greek term for *wanderers*. While all the stars kept their basic relationships and moved slowly as a sphere around the sky, the planets move at differing speeds and change their relationship to the stars as they wander through the zodiac.

The planets have three families, as follows.

The personal planets: The Sun, Moon, Mercury, Venus, and Mars all move fairly quickly, and their signs and relative positions are unique to each personal chart. They symbolize and focus how we relate to each other as individuals in this interpersonal world.

The **social planets:** Jupiter and Saturn spend a longer time in each sign—Jupiter about a year, and Saturn about two and a half years. They describe our social context, the politics and cultural environment of the time, and how we relate to those elements in our chart.

The **generational/transpersonal planets:** Uranus, Neptune, and Pluto can be only seen with a telescope. They move ever slower and describe the bigger issues to face our generation; the metaphysical, psychological, and historical flow of this time in history; and how our chart uniquely relates to that context.

QUALITIES OF THE PLANETS

Sect: Just like many people's dispositions, some planets are more comfortable and stronger in the daytime, while others are stronger at night. If you were born with the Sun above the horizon, your chart is a daylight or diurnal chart. If your Sun is below the horizon, you have a nighttime or nocturnal chart. If a planet is in sect, in their favorite time of the day, it takes a step forward into the foreground of the stage with strength and clarity, while those out of sect take a step back. Sect was considered extremely important in traditional astrology, so we only sort the sect of the traditional planets from the Sun through Saturn. Each sect team, diurnal and nocturnal, has a luminary plus one easy and one challenging planet. Mercury, as usual, is mercurial and changes depending upon circumstances.

Diurnal: Sun, Jupiter, Saturn

Nocturnal: Moon, Venus, Mars

Dignities: These are places where planets are said to be strong. Planets like to be in the sign they rule, and they are considered exalted in a sign that allows their qualities to shine most comfortably. For example, Venus is exalted in Pisces, where it can easily be Venusian: compassionate, creative, sensitive, and receptive. Mars is exalted in Capricorn, where it can easily be muscular, efficient, and organized but can also overdo its natural Mars pushiness. We'll go through this character by character.

Detriment: When a planet is in the sign opposite the one it rules, it is considered in detriment, or uncomfortable. For instance, Venus rules Taurus and Libra, and therefore is in detriment in Aries and Scorpio. But we can all grow from our discomfort: a planet in its detriment will not act pure to its type but can bring interesting breadth to the chart. Venus rules Libra, and therefore is in detriment in Aries, where it produces a nonstandard Venus, a fierce, assertive, and brave heart.

Exalted: Each planet has a sign where it feels most itself, most extreme in its expression. Venus is at its most delicate, aesthetic, Venusian sensitivity in Pisces. A planet is strong in its exalted sign and can become almost too much, a caricature of itself, unless it builds in the opposite strength.

Fall: Each planet is considered in its fall, or in its least comfortable circumstance, like a bull in a china shop, when it is in the sign opposite its exaltation. The Venus that is exalted in Pisces is in its fall in Virgo. Here the mind and heart stay intertwined.

THE CHARACTERS: THE PLANETS

The planets in your chart reflect internalized archetypes; each symbolizes a part of your personality. Anything you can remember or research about the Greek myths will give you a taste of those archetypes. Western astrology leans into the Greek and Roman myths because they are familiar, psychologically complex, and offer a common dialect for us to share. They give us wonderful stories that show the challenging, practical, and positive sides expressed by each planet. They can help you know your options.

It's well worth investigating these same archetypes in mythologies from around the globe, particularly those that influenced your personal ancestors. They are remarkably similar, though each version shares a secret about how that archetype expresses. All those deities often got themselves into trouble. They are patrons of some unique pragmatic work, and they have special talents and gifts to bestow.

For example, the goddess Venus could set hearts on fire. She was a sucker for compliments or gifts, and loyalty wasn't her forte, but she breathed charm, endowed the arts, and opened hearts. Mars fought about anything and everything, but he bestowed strength and virility to humans, animals, and crops, and trained heroes and was a lover to Valor and Venus.

Mercury was not always honest. He was the God of thieves as well as fleet-footed brilliant communicator and messenger of the Gods. I will touch on the myths here but won't go into detail as those stories are well covered in other books and are a great place to start your own research. I will list a few in the further reading section at the end.

Each planet covers their version of a spectrum from a challenging side, through the practical component, and finally to their divine gifts. Some planets have a more challenging expression, like Saturn or Pluto, others a more charming and benefic side, like Venus and Jupiter, but all contain this range of expression in the characteristics of its sign.

To further understand the personalities of the planets, it's helpful to look at their astronomical story as well as their mythologies and notice how they symbolically mirror one another. Saturn, the planet of boundaries, is known for its surrounding ring. Jupiter, planet of abundance, is larger than all the other planets put together, though no one knew that when the planet was named.

For each planetary character, read its spectrum to know how it operates in your chart. Then imagine it clothed in the characteristics of its sign. Read up on the astronomical story and key mythic story for more depth to the symbol. Chew on all these metaphors and patterns when you think of their role in your psyche.

THE PERSONAL PLANETS

Mercury: Messenger

If you're feeling dull and need to wake up your mind, need to think faster, or need to think outside the box, walk with Mercury. Imagine that you are as fast as lightning: move quickly, see clearly, and speak eloquently. Conversely, if you feel too buzzed, as if your nervous system is stretched thin, meditate with your Mercury and ask your mind what it needs to become calm and clear, like a spring-fed pool.

Mercury is the patron saint of the modern world; there is a statue of Mercury on top of Grand Central Station. It symbolizes how we come to know things, how we communicate and connect through our thoughts, words, and nervous systems, and through our technology and movement. Mercury zips around the Sun in 77 days and forms such a tight circle around the Sun that we always see them dancing together, with Mercury either in the same sign, the one before, or the one after the Sun. This is why Mercury was named the mythological messenger of the Sun God and all the Gods in Greek and Roman mythology. This messenger carries the divine thoughts Earthward.

The planet Mercury is indeed mercurial; the effects of this planet change greatly depending upon the sign it shines through and the planets it coordinates with by aspect. Mercury is versatile. In fact, it is hermaphroditic—considered both male and female—and is comfortable in either a daytime or nighttime chart, a chart above or below the horizon. It is most active in the signs it rules—Gemini and Virgo—and is exalted in Virgo. Here Mercury can be its pure type: busy, intelligent, analytical, nervy, aware, and potentially anxious.

Mercury is considered in its fall in Pisces (opposite Virgo), where it proceeds through emotions and visualizations before it analyzes, and is debilitated in Sagittarius (opposite Gemini), where the mind can be brilliant but diffuse, with a wide-ranging scope but less focus. Brilliant people with a debilitated Mercury might have unusually complex minds. They're less particular and articulate but are good at synthesizing information with their senses and keeping their minds integrated with the heart and body.

Mercury appears to back up—or turn retrograde—for three weeks, three times a year. Mercury retrograde is probably the most widely known astrological phenomenon in popular culture because our world is so mercurial, so based on communication, adaptation, and transportation, that we really notice when it's working sideways. Modern life can get a bit complicated, and Mercury retrograde asks us to slow down and pay more attention. Keep a good book with you to read when the subway breaks down. It's a time to review the past, remember, revisit, edit, recollect, reconnect, retreat, renew, and rejuvenate. If you were born under a retrograde

Mercury, you may think or express differently than others, and that could be to your advantage. You may also feel like you're carrying a project or story through from another life. **Challenge:** Mercury is all about the nervous system. The place and quality of your Mercury describes what makes you anxious, what winds you up. When your Mercury is taxed, you can anxiously overthink and imagine all the things that could go wrong or use your mind as an escape pod and hide in a book, in a daydream, or in other people's business to keep your mind busy so you don't have to deal with your heart or gut.

In Greek and Roman mythology, Mercury was also God of thieves whose first act was to steal a musical instrument from his father, Apollo, the Sun. Minds can be tricky, and Mercury can point to that coyote part of your mind that can justify or rationalize your unconscious behavior, hopes, and fears. Mercury describes what distracts and clouds your mind and what sends your nervous systems on strike or leads you into obsession or depression.

Practical: Mercury describes your mental switchboard, how you learn, take in information, and express your thoughts. It can describe how you drive, dance, and move through your world. A good look at the Mercury of a friend or client can tell you how they hear best, what they find funny, and how to communicate with them. Look to Mercury's sign, house, and aspects for clues to help you feel most comfortable communicating.

Gift: Mercury says if you just keep thinking, talking, and imagining possibilities, which are all Mercurial powers, potential is limitless. The God Mercury acted as the messenger of the Gods when they worked for divine purpose, and as a psychopomp, the creature who could dive deep into the underworld and retrieve lost souls. Your Mercury can help you dive deep within your conscious and unconscious mind to therapeutically explore the realms of the psyche. Call on your Mercury to help you integrate your intellect with your heart and life experience and turn intelligence into wisdom. Meditation trains a busy mercurial mind to calm the buzz and become a clearer channel for Spirit. Shamanic journeywork, prayer, and spiritually centered forms of divination can help you listen to the One and live in the presence of divinity.

Explore: Look at the sign of your Mercury, the house it sits within, and the house it rules. Think about the nature of your mind, how you think, how you learn, and whether you obsess restlessly at two in the morning or dream deeply, and contemplate how Mercury expresses itself to that sign.

Affirmation: "Through the gift of Mercury, I come to know my own mind and speak my truth. With Mercury's help I swiftly adapt and respond. I move."

Mercury through the Signs

Mercury in Mars-ruled Aries adds speed and vigor to thinking, and honesty and directness to communication. You can speak spontaneously and confront difficulties. With this Mercury you can miss subtleties or impatiently interrupt because you think you know what's about to be said; though you are often right, you can jump to faulty conclusions. Your jokes can be pointed, direct, and impatient. Choose to ask a wider range of questions and empathize with people with different gifts, especially those who move more slowly or think differently than you do.

Mercury in Venus-ruled Taurus steadies the mind and adds stubbornness and an earthy practicality to thinking. Mercury in Taurus wants tactile examples to understand the process and purpose of what it learns, but then remembers and retains what you learn. This Mercury can add poetry to your words, music to your voice, and earthiness to your humor, particularly after a good meal or when your senses are fed. It can add grounding, even stubbornness, to your opinions. Give yourself the time to learn at your own pace. **Mercury in its own sign of Gemini** speeds up the mind and adds nerviness and a sparkling scintillation. Your Mercury in Gemini is often clever and inventive, funny, and able to talk to a wide range of people, but your thoughts and words can run ahead of your compassion. This Mercury can run swiftly over the surface, allow you to learn easily, multitask, translate comfortably, and see the web of connections, but other aspects need to add depth, empathy, and concentration.

Mercury in Moon-ruled Cancer loans sensitivity to the thinking process but objectivity can be a challenge. Mercury in Cancer can give you good gut intuition, literally: the nervous system affects your digestion. You could be a wonderful storyteller, compassionate if easily defensive, and your memory might be uneven but powerful; if you can remember how you felt, you can remember what happened. Your thoughtful, heart-connected mind benefits from structure and training to help you access a hawk's-eye overview when you need it.

Mercury in Sun-ruled Leo brings a rich, charismatic, entertaining communications style and can make you a great teacher or orator; you can create a great plot and tell a good story. With Mercury in Leo, you can think expansively and kindly, but you may have trouble walking a mile in another person's shoes. You may be open-minded until you form an opinion, and then can stubbornly dig in your heels. If you find yourself thinking you are at the center, that it's all about you, or it's all your fault, gently laugh at yourself and stand back to see the bigger picture.

Mercury in its own sign of Virgo offers a sharp, rigorous, curious intellect, though you could be prone to overthinking. With Mercury in Virgo, you can be a versatile and inventive thinker, perceptive and with a good sense of persuasive logic, and good at law and analysis. Your sense of humor is sharp and funny but occasionally biting and self-deprecating. You can be brilliant at teasing others about their faults. Your busy mind can get anxious or edgy when you don't have something constructive to chew on, so it behooves you to ask good questions. Your mind and body can work together; if your nerves affect your health, consider calming meditation and healthy visualization to get back on track. Under stress, list what is working, what's right with the world, and who supports you.

Mercury in Venus-ruled Libra can speak with a melodious voice and words to paint a picture. Mercury in Libra encourages an open mind and helps you understand others' point of view, which makes you a great diplomat or counselor but could also make clear and easy decisions challenging. You can find non sequiturs hilarious, appreciating the humor in what is out of whack in the world. Although you're willing to work hard toward a more just world, direct confrontation can make you anxious. To learn a new topic, you need to see how it fits in the bigger picture and how it will affect people. Develop your critical thinking so you can balance your naturally optimistic view with an awareness of the needed work.

Mercury in Mars- and Pluto-ruled Scorpio adds to your focus, but that focus can turn into obsession under stress, so direct this Mercury with care. You can express yourself with pointed dark humor, sarcasm, ingenuity, and intensity. Question your suspicions; look for objective facts. Paradoxically, both personally private but deeply curious about other people, you play your cards close to your chest and can hold secrets for others but want to look under every rock and study the worst-case scenarios. Great at research, you love a mystery, but when you develop an opinion, it can be hard to change your mind. Direct confrontation does not work. To use this Mercury with grace, keep your mind open and stay curious about other people's perspective.

Mercury in Jupiter-ruled Sagittarius shoots from the hip; your communication style is frank, open, often ruthlessly honest but without an intentional sting. You can waltz right past social conventions and get away with saying truth that other people might flinch from speaking. You can unintentionally insult other people unless you keep your heart connected. Because you are inherently honest, you can miss clues that other people are not honest or not enough with themselves to be honest with you. You connect across cultural barriers and with the natural world; your philosophic mind wants to travel in all ways possible. You may have bookshelves covering a wide variety of topics. You can pick up accents and languages and talk to people from all socioeconomic classes with ease. Your wide-ranging, always-learning, globally oriented mind can potentially have trouble concentrating or staying on target. Study further; train those flexible mental muscles.

Mercury in Saturn-ruled Capricorn is thoughtful, not a lightweight. If you have Mercury in Capricorn you usually think through what you're going to say before speaking, you like to sound in control and feel organized and secure. You think critically, even scientifically, but may have trouble letting things go or flow. You can write well with a strong sense of sequential order—a beginning, middle, and end. Your thought process tends to be skeptical and specific, but you may need to learn to relax, take your time, and respect a more creative, spontaneous, intuitive approach. When you are worried, you can hold on and obsess over a process for distraction. You can't tell your mind to just drop it, so to let go of work or other serious concerns, you may find it helpful to focus on a more personal craft or project instead.

Mercury in Saturn and Uranus-ruled Aquarius adds an open-minded, observing, outgoing, inclusive perspective. You need to know why you're learning something, how it fits into the big picture before you can take it in. Because you are farsighted and can be aware of the people in the room, you're good at leading meetings or organizing a team but can find the details challenging. Because you can see far horizons, you may forget to look nearby for more information. You are naturally theoretical, but remember to consciously integrate your personal philosophy with your authentic experiences. If a beloved wants to discuss their feelings or problems, please do not try to talk them out of it; just hold space for them and know that counts.

Mercury in Jupiter and Neptune-ruled Pisces has strong intuition and gets clues in dreams. Mercury in Pisces often indicates a good mind, but you may think in symbols, images, and mind maps versus linear logic—whether you are an artist or scientist. Get an impression first, then follow up with the details and logic. You are naturally empathic and can resent people for making you feel guilty or worried unnecessarily. You may shut down or cry around loud conflict. The more gently a person makes a point, the better you can hear them. You have both strong imagination and good intuition but need to consciously learn the difference between the two.

Venus: Beloved

If your heart is sore or if your romantic life is either too quiet or tumultuous, meditate with Venus. It's also time to walk with Venus if you want to learn to value yourself more or to appreciate all the different forms of beauty and tap into your creative muse. Study her, talk with her, embody her.

Venus symbolizes your heart—what you care about and what you create. Venus points to what you find beautiful, what attracts you, what attracts us to you, how you share affection and compassion, what stimulates your sensuality, and how you feel about yourself and your lovability. By sign, house, and aspect, Venus describes what you value and what you want enough to get you into trouble.

Venus loves the night. She is nocturnal, rules Libra and Taurus, is exalted in Pisces, and is therefore debilitated in their opposite signs of Aries, Scorpio, and Virgo. Because this planet spins inside the orbit of the Earth, and we see her dance connected to the Sun, she can only be two signs before or after the Sun. It takes Venus roughly 225 days to go around the Sun. She turns very slowly backward compared to most other planets, a lovely symbol for how our hearts turn differently from our minds.

One day and one rotation on Venus would be approximately 243 days here on Earth, so one side is hot and the other is cold: a great symbol for our own emotional extremes. Venus is hot! So are we in a creative or cuddly Venusian mood. The atmosphere is acidic and the rock is theorized to be alkaline, which means the planet lives in a sustained chemical reaction, a hot, pink, swirling storm, another great planetary metaphor for our emotions when they are tumultuous. Venus is highly reflective and shines brightly in the night sky. Her symbol appears like a hand-held mirror, a reminder that we need to love ourselves to be able to love others in a balanced way.

Challenge: An overstimulated Venus can set your heart on fire: it can instigate heartache, crimes of passion, love addiction, and material indulgences, as if having enough stuff will fill a void. A dazzled Venus can be shallowly affected by superficial appearances or fall in love quickly, unable to see their person objectively. A wounded Venus can

disconnect one from the heart and leave them depressed—
or furious. When the heart is sore, it can help you to help
another—consider something like volunteering at an animal shelter. Or redirect that passionate Venus energy by
painting or dancing it out.

Practical: Venus signifies all things of heart and art,
what we value and what we find beautiful. Think about
what makes beauty, aside from physical beauty: proportion,
grace, creative process. Then things of emotional and social
beauty, fairness, compassion, respect, kindness, and diplomacy. Look to the sign, house, and aspects for clues about
what you find beautiful, how you perceive beauty in the
world, what you love, and music, dance, and art. All of these
are found in the perception of the beholder; it is our senses
that create value. When you know someone's Venus, you
have clues about their love language, how to flirt with them,
and what they need in romance.

Venus also speaks of fertility—of fruits, flowers, the
birds, and the bees. It speaks of the fertility of our creative
nature, of our ability to produce babies and beauty, to birth
a better world.

Gift: Venus relates to our ability to love, care, and be
generous. Like Libra, the sign she rules, Venus calls us to
walk the Beauty Way—a Navajo concept that speaks about
the power of living in right relations with all sentient beings,
and living balanced with the world and with a compassionate, joyful, peaceful, and respectful heart, with the ground
below you, the sky above you, and all the world around you.
Venus speaks of life as a heart-centered metta meditation;
open your heart and love all beings, including yourself.

*Explore: Notice what sign your Venus sits within and think
about your creative process, your love life, what you find beautiful,*

what helps you feel beautiful, and how you show affection, and notice how this expresses or differs from your Venus.

Affirmation: "With the gift of Venus, I open my heart to healing, love, and my creative muse. I seek the Beauty Way to live in balance with all."

Venus through the Signs

Venus in Mars-ruled Aries: You know who you love and who you hate very quickly. Because your emotional responses are so fast and intense, it can drive you nuts when it takes other people a while to know their own heart. You are drawn to strength, independence, and determination, and want your friends and partners to step up and step in and let you know how they feel. You like an emotional challenge. If someone is too easy or too wishy-washy, you will tend to lose interest. Sometimes you can fall in love with a bully or mistake control for strength until you have confidence in your worth and own heart's direction. You can love a good cause and want to fight the good fight in the world. Sometimes an argument can be your way of showing affection, of engaging intensely. Just be aware that it may not be so for others.

Venus in her own sign of Taurus: You love steadily and sometimes possessively. You are probably a good hugger, cuddly. Your friends may count on you to be their Rock of Gibraltar; they may retreat to your kitchen for tea and sympathy under stress. You love to see beauty, smell beauty, feel touch; you love the richness of the garden. This Venus is a sensualist more than a sexualist, but Mars might add more to this spark. Love for you can be a good meal, a back rub, a leisurely touch, a bill paid. You need time to know a person and warm up, but once you connect, you do not let go of a love or friendship easily. You value loyalty in your friends, beloveds, and those you work with, and offer it in return.

Venus in Mercury-ruled Gemini: This Venus brings a sparkling humor and nervousness to both the heart and to the creative process, and you may have many creative projects going at once. You can usually find the right words to speak to anybody. You need to communicate with your love for your heart to follow. You want to laugh with them, play with them. Words can seduce you and you can seduce with words. This love language of communication can be used in so many ways to enrich your world. You honestly can care about more than one person at a time, though you don't necessarily need to touch them; just remember that this is not so for everyone.

Venus in Moon-ruled Cancer, you need to feel safe to love. Sometimes you might find it easier to express love in a parental way rather than wild romance. When you love someone, you want to be family. You can show your love—and feel loved—through caring, nurturing, and feeling protected or protecting. You may love to cook for the ones you love or feel loved when someone feeds you. Sometimes your beloveds can project their unfinished mother issues upon you, which was not your intention; this needs to be clarified before they rebel instead of work through things with you in partnership. It may take you a while to trust friendship and affection, especially if you've had your feelings hurt, but this is okay; there is no need to justify the time you need. It is good for you and your beloveds to define terms, find out what they mean when they say they care, and express what you mean; make sure you're on the same page.

Venus in Sun-ruled Leo, let no one ignore you. You don't need to be the center of the world, but you do need to be the center of your beloveds' world in both family and romance. In return, you can share that joy by truly centering someone you love and making them feel like they are the only person on Earth, or at least the most wonderful in your eyes. When you love or when you hate, you can express your emotions with panache and drama. Watch that you don't stray too far into hyperbole and lose believability. What will not work for you is to be taken for granted, ignored, or upstaged, and in return you will not do that to someone you love. Appearance matters to you. You understand the grace within your life and others and can bring beauty wherever you go.

Venus in Mercury-ruled Virgo brings particularity to the heart. Deeply compassionate and naturally introspective, you may show the world you love through an interest in the healing arts. You want to see the world improve and grow. Instead of flowers, you may offer a bouquet of great advice, but just make sure people are ready for it. You also can analyze or process a relationship as a way of creating intimacy. Your mind and heart need to work together. You need to understand what's going on, but overprocessing love can be like pulling up carrots to see if they're growing. Sometimes you need to honor the mystery of the evolution of a relationship. Virgo is an Earth sign, you may grow more comfortable in your body and in your affection as the years go by. You do not suffer fools lightly. Although you are drawn to a wild spectrum of types, you are attracted to competence and intelligence, to people who take care of themselves, who understand the problem and are interested in solutions.

Venus in her own sign of Libra is softhearted and can love for the sake of loving. You can love romance and creative processes, enjoy the unset and romantic moments, and may work toward the arts and social justice. You do not enjoy fighting or analysis as a way of connecting, though you may be drawn to those passionate people. At times you'll know more about what the people around you want and need than you do your own desires. Since love needs to be able to work through problems as well as celebrate harmonious moments, find creative ways to mediate differences, to speak up for what you need. Study relationship skills, apply them, and take them on as your superpower. It means a lot to you if your beloveds know what you like and bring you offerings. It is the awareness of you, not the object, that pleases your heart.

Venus in Mars-ruled Scorpio brings passion. That passion could be for a wild affair or for solitude, but no matter which, you are all in or all out. You could feel very little emotional ambiguity. You would hate to have your relationships or friendships talked about by others. It doesn't mean that you're not proud of them, but rather that you need privacy for your heart to open. Sometimes you may prefer not to get involved, because when you do, it wakes up uncomfortably intense primal emotions. You need absolute loyalty from your romantic partners, though sometimes it may be hard to give it back, because then one person could sink you. Clandestine relationships can be tempting unless you are completely honest with yourself about their reciprocal nature. It helps for you to have something to focus upon that is completely within your control, your work, art, or research, someplace to safely put your obsession so you can approach your emotional life with more equanimity and less fear of loss. Once you allow yourself to attach, you can walk into the depths. When you say you will be there for better or worse, you mean it. Although you feel deeply, you may not want to have to show it on a regular basis nor to talk about it often. Still waters run deep.

Venus in Jupiter-ruled Sagittarius brings a playful quality. With your world-beat persona and fear of being trapped, you can fall in love with someone with a foreign accent or a one-way ticket out of town. You will be more willing to walk into a relationship if it stays spacious and exploratory. Physical loyalty isn't a problem for you, but you may hate to feel like someone wants to know where you are every minute. You appreciate when someone brings you something from another culture or with a metaphysical touch. Your heart can open when you are out dancing, with animals, or on a walk in the woods. Sometimes in that far-ranging soul of yours, you may miss the subtle needs of the people nearby. You need and offer honesty, and can be less than tactful in love, but can sometimes miss the subtlety of a deeper truth. Look, listen, and keep exploring.

Venus in Saturn-ruled Capricorn lends control to the feelings. And control can be an issue in your love. Maybe as you were growing up you didn't have room to play. You might have been the oldest or felt emotionally responsible for the people around you. Sometimes, in response to those control issues, you may love to feel out of control, to be drawn to someone competent enough for you to relax and let go. Work at your craft. It will feel good to improve your artistry, and you tend to feel loved when your efforts are appreciated. You may be a bit more reserved than others, but that does not mean your feelings are any less deep. Sometimes, when you love someone, you work harder for them, just when they need your presence and your attention instead. You don't have to fix anything for them. Whether in parenting, love, or career, work on developing relationship skills. Because these skills might be something you needed to learn instead of something inherent to you, you may incorporate them in a unique way and be able to teach others in a way you otherwise would not be able to.

Venus in Saturn-ruled Aquarius can bring an unusual sense of aesthetics and affection. What you find beautiful may be considered odd or eccentric, but it makes you happy. You do well in group situations. Feeling love and affection with your circle of friends or spiritual community can give you the emotional stability to open your heart in intimate relationships. You can bring heart to a team or collective action, in a community or public setting. Watch a tendency to get abstracted from your emotions, like the Moon in Aquarius. When asked how you feel, you may vacillate, saying things like "Well, I think I feel . . ." or "My theory on my feelings is . . ." It can be particularly hard for you to identify a primal emotion that doesn't fit in your philosophy. Jealousy could take you by surprise. Keep the lines of communication open with your beloveds and find out how they feel on a regular basis, because you can miss signals of a problem but will be happy to work to make everyone more comfortable once you know. You do care about the larger community of humankind and can help us take loving action to make this a better world.

Venus in Jupiter and Neptune-ruled Pisces brings dreaminess to the heart. You are likely more aware of the sensitive flow of energy between you and others than they are. Just know that sensitivity is your superpower; it is not that they are being insensitive jerks. You have strong intuition about the people that you love, your family, and all your beloveds; you may imagine your worries and pick up on their real experiences. Pay attention to your dreams and daydreams for information, but always ask rather than assume when your heart worries. Your sense of aesthetics may prefer subtle or uncluttered beauty. You are deeply affected by the aesthetics of your surroundings—the flower on the windowsill, the sound of the meadowlark. The richness of financial worth is not what matters to you, though you may like nice things. You have a sentimental streak and are drawn to people who are strong enough that they can help protect your sensitive nature. It can physically hurt to hear notes out of tune or see ugliness around you.

Mars: Motion

If your tail is twitching; if you find yourself irritable, argumentative, abrupt, accident-prone; or if other people pick fights with you and you wonder why, Mars can help you own and direct your energy flow. Conversely, if you lost your passion and life force, or if you are exhausted or are having trouble setting boundaries, take a brisk walk with Mars and find that spark and edge.

Mars signifies your passion, muscles, willfulness, machismo, entrepreneurial qualities, inner explorer, animus, temper, aggression, and defenses. This includes the cellular defenses of your immune system. Mars points to what triggers you, what ticks you off, but also where you may be called be a hero.

Mars is nocturnal, rules Aries and Scorpio, and is exalted in Capricorn, where it can climb many mountains. It is debilitated in Libra, Taurus, and Cancer, all places where it needs to be softer and more complex in its expression. Mars is the first planet on the far side of the Earth from the Sun, and so its orbit is the fastest-moving one, independent of the Sun. Mars takes about 1.9 Earth years to spin around the zodiac. It appears independent, erratic, spontaneous, and pulses red, which adds to its machismo mystique.

Challenge: If you don't know what you want or don't have a healthy and responsible way to achieve it, your Mars could feel suppressed. If people ignore your boundaries and wishes, your Mars may feel undernourished. A disconnected Mars can leave you exhausted, apathetic, indifferent, passive-aggressive, and potentially depressed. On the other end, an inflamed Mars can produce toxic masculinity (regardless of your gender), fury, bullying, overriding willfulness, and misuse of sexuality. When Mars doesn't have a clear channel for healthy expression, it can leave you feeling accident-prone or belligerent. Because Mars symbolizes your personal standing army, a suppressed or disconnected Mars can make it hard to set boundaries.

Practical: Mars represents muscles, physical prowess (or lack thereof), action, strength, testosterone, muscles, mechanical power, immune system, manual labor, and martial arts. Mars points out where you can be definite, competent, and just get it done. It shows you what you desire and speaks of your sexuality—as opposed to your sensuality—what you crave, what gets you excited. For a country, Mars symbolizes the standing army whose job it is not to run the country but to protect us from invaders. Your immune system functions like a standing army, keeps out the invaders, and helps you stay healthy. Because Mars is so muscular, when we feel that flash of Mars anger, it can help us to go chop wood or hit the punching bag, to break a plate and not a bone. Get the Mars out of the body so it is not stuck in the heart and muscles.

Gift: Mars symbolizes your heroic nature, where you can protect and provide for those who need it. Your Mars can act like a supportive companion who watches your back. It helps you look for brave solutions and find your physical energy, sexuality, passion, and clear understanding of what you want and need. Mars gives you the right to say "yes" and embrace life with passion. Your ability to set healthy boundaries allows you to welcome life intimately. It helps you reach out and act with compassion knowing that you can still take care of yourself in the center.

Affirmation: "By the gift of Mars, my 'yes' can truly mean yes because my 'no' will be heard. I can make healthy decisions and hold clean boundaries."

Mars through the Signs

Mars in Mars-ruled Aries shoots from the hip. You love a challenge, and when you agree to a project or take on an adventure, you do it wholeheartedly. Whatever gender you hold, this is straightforward, charismatic and brave energy, able to catalyze a room or handle a crisis. Just watch the tendency to make a crisis or fight for the sake of fighting, as not everyone loves a recreational argument. Fighting and making up as a part of intimacy can become a habit, unless you find a good fight elsewhere and learn other ways to intensely engage. This Mars can heat up an otherwise-cool chart and pour oil on the flames of a hot chart. Athleticism may be natural to you, and you play to win. If you feel your temper spiking, go chop wood, work out, dance up a storm, or channel your inner hero; use that physicality productively and get it out of your muscles. Attraction and passion can boil up quickly once it's ignited, and you may take an athletic approach to sex. What will really tick off your Mars in Aries is prevarication, wimpiness, repetition, or being told what to do by someone whose competence you do not respect. This Mars wants action; to keep it out of trouble give it worthy work. You can make a heroic first responder, officially or otherwise. You are usually the first one in the room to respond to a crisis or opportunity.

Mars in Venus-ruled Taurus, remember the children's story of Ferdinand the bull, who loved to sit peacefully in his fields? One day a bee stung him, and he leaped all over the place, so the scouts thought he'd be perfect in the bull-fighting ring. But once there, he just contentedly smelled flowers. He would neither budge nor perform. That is Mars in Taurus. You can get ticked off if you are rushed or stung, if you deal with disloyalty, or if someone is sitting in your favorite chair. Once you dig in your heels, there is no moving or persuading you. You need time for a slow ramp-up in the bedroom, time to connect the heart to the body, then time to activate the senses, but after that, you can be a true, delicious sensualist. Watch for a tendency to set boundaries passive-aggressively; own those borders and plant flowers on them, but ask directly for what you want and need. You can be the solid shoulder to cry on. Your sturdy presence can form a heroic bulwark to protect your beloveds.

Mars in Mercury-ruled Gemini brings remarkable adaptable versatility; you can be a jack-of-all-trades. It will tick you off to be given the silent treatment or be told to get to the point while you are telling the story, sketching a beautiful pattern with your words. You may be an external processor and need to get your feelings out and on the table, but you could prefer to do it in bits and pieces, starts and stops, and work with a light touch rather than sit down and negotiate the whole lump at once. You can diffuse with scintillating wit or slice with a verbal rapier; you duel with words. Competition isn't really your thing, but bicycling, dance, fencing, and yoga can all be wonderful ways for you to engage the body. You can also seduce with words and need a variety of experience, not necessarily a variety of people, in your love life. You can get people talking who normally don't and help people find the words or express their story for them as actor, counselor, editor, arbitrator, journalist, mediator, or anywhere people need to understand and feel heard.

Mars in Moon-ruled Cancer, safety is seductive to you. You need to know that your heart is safe to take emotional risks and reach out. A cozy bed, the comforts of home, a cat happy to see you—you love to be loved. When you don't feel safe, your defenses can be spectacular. Your emotions can feel soft and squishy on the inside, which is why you can be like the crab and become hard with claws on the outside. Mars in Cancer can be found in military geniuses who defend their country. It can really tick you off to feel teased, critiqued, or unsupported by your home team. When you feel unhappy or angry, you can swallow your feelings, and this could affect your gut; take good care of your digestive system and find ways to identify and express those feelings in another way. If your body knows you are listening, it may be less likely to act up. You may not be particularly interested in highly competitive sports, as you hate to lose, but could love to swim, hike, or have a good snowball fight. You can put great energy into improving or protecting the home or homeland and heroically protect the unhoused and unfed.

Mars in Sun-ruled Leo, what a big heart you have. You can operate with generosity and care, and you have an electric charisma ready to shine for the benefit of all you do. When you tap into your Mars in Leo, you can be the quintessential extrovert who can light up a room and is energized when engaging the public. You love a little pomp and circumstance, a bit of velvet in the bedroom. When you love, you love generously and take good care of others. It will be easier for you to engage in any sport or movement that has a performance element. You can work well in a team sport as long as you occasionally shine in the center. You will always respect someone for loving you. You don't play hard to get unless they lose focus. What can really tick you off is being ignored or asked to settle for less. When you get mad, you plant your feet and roar. Your leonine heart can operate with the power of a leader, and a good monarch can heroically take care of who they feel responsible for. Tap into that generous Leo heart.

Mars in Mercury-ruled Virgo, much to the surprise of others, you can be deliciously embodied. Though, sometimes you need to be called back out of your head and into your body, so dance first, touch, move together. Once you are in your body, you know what to do. You may also be sapiosexual, attracted to intelligence, but just make sure that intelligence is also connected to heart and interested in good relationship skills. Since you are always improving yourself, you don't need much feedback from others. You've probably already thought of their complaint. If someone lightly states a problem, you'll do your best to fix it, but you can get an allergic, defensive reaction if blame is tossed about. For you, fault-finding destroys love. Stupidity ticks you off, and so does being told not to think or talk about a problem; you need to process until you're good and ready. Conspiracy theories can infuriate you, as you want to be a bountiful fountain of healthy, well-researched information. You may love to dance or enjoy yoga or body-centered prayer—any pursuit where health and Spirit mix. You can be a natural healer both through the energy of your hands and an ability to diagnose problems.

Mars in Venus-ruled Libra, you have a complex Mars. Here Mars and Venus work together, but sometimes at cross-purposes. It is important for you to know what you want and need as much as you know what others desire. You want to be wanted; another person's desire for you can be mesmerizing. Romance, that liminal moment of two beings in attraction, can be addictive, both artistically and interpersonally. Unnecessary ugliness can tick you off, a painting crooked on the wall calls you to straighten it, but you will get most upset over an unjust, unfair situation, particularly a false accusation. While you can fight the good fight for truth, justice, and equity, it hurts to be around conflicts between people you love. You may not be particularly athletically inclined but can dance the night away. It can be active as long as the athleticism is mixed with Venusian grace. Under stress you want to feel connection with your beloveds or your team; there is no problem you can't handle if you feel the relationship connection first.

Mars in Mars- and Pluto-ruled Scorpio. You smolder. Mars in Scorpio can feel like a glowing coal underneath the ashes. Once it's stirred up, it can ignite conflagrations of either passion or anger. When you get angry, you can either snap out with a sharp scorpion stinger or implode and withhold; in either case, the mess may be hard to clean up. Learn your warning signs and catch yourself before you get that mad. Take some time out to cool off, then be honest about those very strong primal feelings that are your gift and trouble. You may be drawn to challenging relationships, partly as an excuse to get the solitude you need as well as the intense connection you crave, unless you negotiate for occasional solitude. You like to win and can be a fierce competitor who practices obsessively but may choose not to enter that fray. No one should try to bamboozle or lie to you because you can see right through it, and once your trust is broken, it takes a long time, if ever, to repair. Before you plot revenge, which can be an art form for you, trust karma to handle it and refocus on your own path. Your superpower can be to ferret out the mysteries. You tend to win the fights you get in, but it can get messy, so choose your fights carefully and use that power for good. We need your ability to stand up for the world's injustices.

Mars in Jupiter-ruled Sagittarius, the old Texan song "Don't Fence Me In" is your theme; you need lots of room, open doors, and to always feel you have choice. Although you are outspoken and direct, you don't like to perseverate in an argument. Some people might take you as flighty, but you may want to keep the flow moving rather than drill down on that problem. Your mood tends to be resilient. You don't anger easily unless you feel trapped or lied to. Movement helps you process, so if you need to talk over a tricky subject, walk side by side rather than confront directly across the table. Movement suits you. You may be a hell of a runner or bicyclist; you may ride horses or run with your dogs. Even in a video game, you would hate to lose a race. You may be attracted to people while you travel, people who come from another culture or socioeconomic class, people who can broaden your world experience. You tend to ignore conventions and are not trapped by the opinions of others. You have the ability to reinvent the system to work more cleanly and can stand up for the underdog in so many situations.

Mars in Saturn-ruled Capricorn is considered exalted; this is a powerful Mars with places to go and things to do. Think carefully about what success means to you. This Mars wants to accomplish, to climb that mountain and be the best at whatever profession, sport, or goal matters to you and helps you be tenaciously determined in the process. It behooves you to map your short-term goals on the way to achieve your long-term mountains. Depression hovers and anger rumble if you feel your work is not taken seriously or if someone stands in your way. If you don't have good models from your own childhood, look for mentors to help you climb those mountains. You rather like being in control of your circumstances and can either be attracted to strength in another or are happy to run the scenario. Your managerial skills are powerful. People who need them will bless you. You can make the trains run on time or set up triage in a crisis. You may be both honored and ticked off at being taken for granted by people who assume you can fix or do anything. People who did not ask for your advice will resist you. Your family and beloveds may often just want your presence.

Mars in Saturn-ruled Aquarius, you can work a room. You get a major energetic exchange at a meeting, team sport, movie set, party, performance, political rally, or festival where your ability to reach everyone in the room comes alive. When you feel like it, you can infuse a group with enthusiastic team spirit and help them all feel part of the glow. Some Mars in Aquarius can create a community of thoughts and ideas—rather than of people—and get energy from their work. Sexual chemistry is delightful but rarely drives you; you can like the idea of group sex, but for the most part, you need friendship first. Your best beloveds could occasionally feel you are looking over their shoulder at the larger audience and wonder if they are enough for you. One who loves you will understand that you need both someone to come home to and someone to see you launch. You need your beloveds not to feel possessive but have your back in those large groups and help you return to your own heart at the end of the day. It will really tick you off to feel isolated, limited, or bored. You can be a true hero for your people, whatever community connects with your identity.

Mars in Jupiter-ruled Pisces, you can hold your ground with the best but do not like expectations to be aggressive in an argument or the bedroom. Sensitive, thoughtful, naturally receptive, empathic, and able to tune in to what others need, you hate to feel guilty and so can block your empathy if it will pull you into a dark space. For you, exercise is about creating sculpture, refining form, and feeling strong and beautiful. Your senses are alive; music, scent, and atmosphere all affect you deeply. You understand the gift of fantasy and can let your mind take you to beautiful places. It can really tick you off to see anyone mistreated or when the people around you don't take care of themselves, because you will feel their pain. You can heroically go to bat for the underdog, the underappreciated, the underrepresented. When you're mad, though there can be dramatic flares, you'll tend to withdraw or flood with tears, or guilt-trip, rather than just go on the attack. But you'd prefer to find a subtle way through the problem. You have a special rapport with animals and can communicate without words; their presence, whether the squirrel in the park or the cat on the lap, can be restful after a busy day.

THE SOCIAL PLANETS

Jupiter spends about a year in a sign, and Saturn about two and a half years. You share these positions with all the people born around your year. Jupiter and Saturn describe your social context, the politics and cultural environment of the time, and how you relate to those elements in our chart.

Look at the sign of your Jupiter and Saturn, think about the other planets they interact with by aspect in your chart, and contemplate your experience with authority, personal and external, your work, and your relationship to generosity, luck, and expansion.

Jupiter: Abundance

Jupiter offers resources, a place in your chart with the potential for liberal abundance, optimism, and expansion. It symbolizes how you form and expand your world through travel and a global perspective; through education, law, philosophy, abundance, spirit, and generosity; and through your ability to see the bigger picture.

Jupiter loves the day, it rules Sagittarius and Pisces, and is exalted in Cancer, all places where it's expansiveness can overflow. It is debilitated in the opposite signs of Gemini, Virgo, and Capricorn, particular signs or ones with boundaries. Jupiter is huge: even though it looks about the same size as Venus in the night sky, its volume is one and a half times that of all the other planets put together. It symbolizes abundance, for better or worse. When Jupiter challenges one of the parental planets—the Moon or Saturn—it can signify an overbearing parent who put their needs ahead of child's. Jupiter spends approximately a year in each sign and takes 12 years to go around the zodiac. Many cultures felt its enormity, appreciated its regularity, and named it after their most prominent God.

Challenge: Jupiter's abundance can become excess. It can signify too much, overindulgence, overeating, overwhelm, arrogance, unhealthy growth, or that odd magical thinking that counts on luck rather than work. It can signal toxic positivism, a Pollyanna-like avoidance of the shadow, unless you choose to see the whole picture. Jupiter encourages you to be generous, but it can also nudge you to do too much for others and create codependence through enabling. If Jupiter is strongly connected to your Sun or ascendant, it can signal a dominant personality, which could overshadow the needs and subtleties of others, unless you choose to engage empathy and use that scope for good. If Jupiter is disconnected, limited, or relates to the seventh or eighth house, you can feel like others have abundance but you do not, and that others are lucky and you are not, unless you own your Jupiter and create a conscious connection with its potential.

Practical: Jupiter helps make your world bigger—it signifies publication and broadcasting, getting the word out, and philosophizing. You can look to Jupiter for where luck and joy can enter your life. Here your healthy generosity can create a generous flow back toward you.

Gift: Jupiter symbolizes freedom and expansion. Look to your Jupiter for a hawk's-eye view on the situation, to stand high up on a mountaintop and take in the whole scene, the bigger picture. Jupiter can add a metaphysical perspective and help you see your situation from a philosophic, karmic perspective. Transiting Jupiter can help free you from a tangled situation and help you see beyond the present constraints, though you need to find a practical way to implement the solution. Here you can be larger than life. Jupiter can bring you to your place of gratitude, and in that gratitude, help you find hope.

Meditation: If your world just feels too small and rigid, or your efforts feel insignificant, if gratitude is fugitive, walk with Jupiter and expand your horizons and your heart. Take a walk and feel yourself slowly expanding, growing bigger as your energy field expands beyond your body to fill the space and move in a steady, noble pattern. Feel how much you have to offer the world. There are no limits.

Affirmation: "I am enough, I have enough, and I can generously share in any circumstance."

Jupiter through the Signs

Jupiter in Mars-ruled Aries adds impulsiveness, directness, spark, and fire. You can bring the heat or burn down the house. Routine is hard for you; you invent and create whole new paths and will do it your way. Spontaneous moments can bring you joy.

Jupiter in Venus-ruled Taurus adds gravitas and solidness. You bring the grounding; depending upon your choice, you can be materialistic or materially generous. Feeling comfortable in your world with a solid home base gives you the freedom to expand.

Jupiter in Mercury-ruled Gemini brings an extra ability to communicate and may grow up with too much information. Words flow from you and can bring inspiring messages or they can diffuse as they scatter; you need to bring a focus and purpose for all the many thoughts.

Jupiter in Moon-ruled Cancer brings oceanic emotions. Your feelings roll in great waves like the North Atlantic, and you can let them expand your art, consciousness, and heart, or feel swamped by them. Your creative process and warm heart can feed the world. You get by giving and nurturing on the cosmic level.

Jupiter in Sun-ruled Leo can bring an expansive presence, which could get you in trouble when you're young but grows more comfortable as you mature. The house where Jupiter dwells can be where you take your space, where you feel distant horizons and can let yourself shine.

Jupiter in Mercury-ruled Virgo brings thoughtful self-refinement. This inner voice may say that if you just improve, fix, refine, and grow, you will be free. And you can offer that same view to those around you, whether or not they want to hear it. You will always evolve your craft. Just celebrate every step of progress along the way.

Jupiter in Venus-ruled Libra can believe that relationships can set you free, which can be addictive but also magical as long as your first relationship is with yourself and with Spirit and you liberate the other person as well as yourself with this gift.

Jupiter in Mars and Pluto-ruled Scorpio adds a belief in the transformative power of extremes. It's up to you to choose which extremes and how you want to transform. It can bring a muskiness and sex appeal to be used with respect.

Jupiter in its own sign of Sagittarius can bring an internal flotation device that can help in any storm, a thread of optimism that can lead you forward and act like a guardian angel. It's up to you not to tire out your angels. Be willing to put in the work to make it so.

Jupiter in Saturn-ruled Capricorn imparts the belief that work can set you free, as long as you are the one who guides the work you do. The serious leadership and determination of Jupiter and Capricorn can also leave you feeling like if you don't do it, nobody will, and it won't get done. Rather than dominate, choose to collaborate with all sentient beings.

Jupiter in Saturn- and Uranus-ruled Aquarius brings a connection to the public and a personality that expands to fill the room. You may feel a responsibility to the larger collective and be a minister or leader to your circle, family, group, or community. This is a gift if you believe it can be as liberating for that larger circle as it is for you.

Jupiter in Jupiter and Neptune-ruled Pisces believes in the freeing power of sacrifice. You bring the gift of all of yourself to what you do, but you don't have to give yourself away in the process. This Jupiter connects you to Spirit, intuition, to the more-than-earthly realms; if you don't get lost out of that portal but can instead be that doorway for those luminous realms into this world, what a gift.

Saturn: Structure

If your life feels disorganized or unstructured and you could use some clear boundaries and organization, work with your Saturn. Conversely, if you feel like other people know what they're doing or have the authority, and you don't, walk with Saturn and let Saturn loan you strength. In your mind's eye, reach into your elder self, imagine the wise one within, your future-most adult and mature persona, and ask how they would handle the situation.

Saturn asks you to buck up and deal, to be an adult. If you don't take responsibility for your life and build up the skills you need for your direction, other people will do it for you and tell you what to do. Saturn speaks about your relationship to authority and structure, both around you and within you. It refers to what you don't have as a baby but grow over time: bones, teeth, maturity, boundaries, structure, discipline, learning through experience, personal authority, and, eventually, wisdom. It also symbolizes foundations, restrictions, ancestors, and external authority, and how you are affected by your father's lineage. It loans gravitas, seriousness, and a tendency to worry to whatever planet it touches by aspect.

Saturn is diurnal. It rules Capricorn and Aquarius, and is exalted in Libra. It is debilitated and less strong in the opposite signs of Cancer, Leo, and Aries. Saturn is known for that wonderful visible band, the boundary around the planet. It is the farthest planet visible to the naked eye and was once known as the boundary of our solar system. Saturn takes about 29 and a half years around the zodiac, and every time it aspects itself by a challenging aspect (around 7 years, 14 years, 21 years, and 29 years old, when Saturn returns to its natal place, and then approximately every 7 and one third years for the rest of our lives), we often face challenges that may be a pain at the time but help us grow confidence in our skills and discipline and insist we step into our personal authority. We mature.

Challenge: Saturn can challenge you with a limited reality. An unloving Saturn can manifest as abusive authority, power struggles, and a desire for power over others to handle one's own insecurity. An under-activated Saturn can leave you stuck in the feeling that everybody else has skills, control, ability, power, and you do not. If you do not have a good, healthy, empowering model for authority, it can be challenging to walk into your own Saturn power, and you may have to go on a search for people who use that power well. Saturn concerns honor and responsibility, so if you do something that violates your honor that is irresponsible, Saturn will come get you and hold you to task. When Saturn activates, you get a chance to mature, but that can also leave you feeling old, creaky, brittle, or discouraged until you embrace this new level of maturity and look for the worth within. You will feel younger when the transit passes, but with that new level of knowing.

Practical: Saturn helps us build the capacities to organize, structure, administer. It speaks of all structures in our lives, whether that is corporate hierarchy or family patterns, or the rules and disciplines that help us organize our lives. It governs laws and the way those laws and rules are enforced. These forms are not inherently bad or good; their worth is entirely dependent on how and why they are implemented. Saturn symbolizes those practical structures of the bones of our house, skeletons, and teeth. We cannot grow taller than our skeleton provides, but it is what holds us up. Because Saturn rules what matures over time, it speaks of the beauties and the problems of the aging process. To engage a good Saturn, learn a craft and develop personal discipline to accomplish your goals.

Gift: Saturn is your power within, the wise elder you can tap into. When you're young, the gift of Saturn can be modeled by teachers, parents, elders, and keepers of the law; you learn what it is to take things seriously and walk into your competence. You grow your personal authority by challenging others in your teenage years, as Saturn opposes your natal Saturn at 14 years. The world says you're an adult at 21, when Saturn squares Saturn. You practice your adulthood from 21 until your Saturn return, when Saturn comes back to where it was when you were born when you are around 29. Now your brain is fully formed. You are now wired to be aware of consequence. When you are over 30, you are in the next generation, the generation making the rules and doing the work. Now it is up to you to build and revise the structures of our society. Throughout your life Saturn speaks to you like a martial arts sensei, the teacher without and the teacher within, nudging your soul into responsible growth.

Affirmation: "*The strength of my bones supports my body. The walls of my house keep me safe. Through the power of Saturn I learn to respect boundaries, structures, limits, the wisdom of the elders, and the ripening elder within me.*"

Saturn through the Signs

Saturn in Mars-ruled Aries imparts a dynamic sense of personal authority. You can both question and rebel from all authority and yet long to find, or be, a leader who knows what they're doing. You do not like to be controlled by others, particularly by people who misuse their authority, but understand the need for chain of command. Use your own control and power for good.

Saturn in Venus-ruled Taurus, your authority can be found in your tenacity, your ability to hold your ground in the center like a rooted tree. You may have a fear of other people owning your resources. Like a tree, it can be uncomfortable for you to move. You need to root deep again in a new identity, place, or process to feel your strength. Be flexible and strong like a pine tree waving in the wind.

Saturn in Mercury-ruled Gemini loans authority to your words and strength to your nervous system. You may be afraid of missing out, of not being in the know. You may feel more secure when your information is organized, though your organizational system may be unique.

Saturn in Moon-ruled Cancer can lead you to feel like a universal parent, but what that means depends on your experience of parenting as a child. This Saturn can bring a fear of insecurity. Do you nurture and protect, or do you control them for their own good? First parent yourself the way you wish you had been parented and then channel that into the world around you.

Saturn in Sun-ruled Leo can make it seem important to be seen as a unique leader. This can be dangerous in interpersonal dynamics or politics if you want to be seen as a leader without truly caring about those you lead. But it works beautifully in an art form or profession where you have earned the chops. You may have a fear of being invisible or mediocre. Contemplate healthy leadership and empower those around you.

Saturn in Mercury-ruled Virgo can really sweat the details. This Saturn needs to look at worst-case scenarios and know that all contingencies can be dealt with. You can be afraid to miss that one important detail. Worrying about something is not the same thing as just doing it. This can make you a phenomenal project manager on any scale, but watch a tendency to micromanage yourself and others; trust competence and the core goal.

Saturn in Venus-ruled Libra can help you be one half of a power couple; relationships expand you and help you use that Saturn empowerment for the good of all. Maybe your partner is your creative muse, and you can add Saturn's structure to hearts and art and create great beauty. But this Saturn can also leave you afraid to be controlled by love or attachment and so become controlling yourself or choose to opt out to keep your self-control. Develop that heart-centered power within and share it with others.

Saturn in Mars and Pluto-ruled Scorpio can bring some interesting control issues both around sexuality and behind the scenes in any organization. You have a fear of shallowness, of people poking into your personal business, and of being stuck without the potential to evolve. You know secrets, whether in the therapeutic context or in a power-brokering way and are drawn to transformative work; make a positive transformation.

Saturn in Jupiter-ruled Sagittarius can bring a fear of being trapped or caught, limited or cornered, and a belief that truth shall set you free. You'd rather not get caught in the muck underneath the problem but can lead people to a broader horizon. Stay aware of what you want to run toward, not what you are running away from.

Saturn in Saturn-ruled Capricorn adds organization and systems to your chart. It can add essential structure to a chart of air and water or tense control to an already-efficient chart. A competent scientific or professional mind can slide into obsessive-compulsion under stress. Your fear may be that you are stuck going nowhere. It is important for you to feel good about your work, to have your work respected, and to feel that you are making progress.

Saturn in Saturn and Uranus-ruled Aquarius adds a pleasant dispassion, an ability to stand back, to see the room and see what needs to be done. This supports professional work but can put a cramp in your love life. Your rhythms and routines make sense to you, but you may look at more emotionally driven people and wonder what they're doing. You could be wary of an emotionally intense, erratic, and incompetent world. You work well within professional systems, but remember systems should work for you rather than you needing to work for a system.

Saturn in Jupiter and Neptune-ruled Pisces imparts an archetype of vulnerability. People born your year can be unusually aware of vulnerability, emotional vulnerability, economic vulnerability, spiritual vulnerability, and see both the danger and the need for the world to be a safer place and the compassion that comes from this awareness of other people's vulnerability as much as your own.

THE GENERATIONAL TRANSPERSONAL PLANETS

These planets can only be seen with a telescope—they move even slower and describe the bigger issues to face our generation; the metaphysical, psychological, and historical flow of this time in history; and how your chart uniquely relates to that environment.

You share the same sign for these planets with all the other people born during that cycle; Uranus spends about 7 years in a sign, Neptune almost 14 years, and Pluto averages over 20 years in a sign. What will be unique in your chart is how those planets relate to the other planets, what planets they aspect and comingle their energies with, and what house it dwells in and affects the most.

Think about your transpersonal planets—Uranus, Neptune, and Pluto. What houses do they occupy? What planets do they interact with? Contemplate the psychic, cultural, and emotional milieu of your generation. Notice where electric revolutionary possibilities come into your life, how you respond to Spirit, the numinous, that which is beyond reality, and how you deal with that the dynamics of power, intensity, and rebirth.

Uranus: Change

If you are ready to make a major change and need some healthy chaos, Uranus can help you break the barriers and bring the spark. Conversely, if your life is already chaotic and you need help finding purpose and direction, this planet can help create a fresh path. Imagine dipping into that primordial chaotic potential. Call in Uranus and what is needed to enliven your life, and watch your whole life change.

Uranus symbolizes change, difference, excitement, revolution, electricity. It describes how you work outside of the box and how comfortable you are with those who live beyond ordinary bounds. Uranus speaks of the iconoclast, electricity, eccentricity, change, invention, mechanization, and transformation.

This planet is the modern co-ruler of Aquarius and is debilitated in Leo. It's the third-largest planet and takes 84 years around the zodiac but spins through its day in about 17 hours. It has symbolized change since it was first seen with new telescopes in 1781. It's discovery radically altered our concept of the solar system. It broke open our understanding and brought a new astronomical truth. That is what Uranus offers to us by transit. Uranus spins in a different orientation than other planets, tilted with one pole pointing toward the Sun, which creates a unique and wild electrical field around the planet. The wacky orbit, its electricity, and its role as a doorway into new understanding offer wonderful metaphors for how Uranus works in your chart. Whatever planet interacts with Uranus in your chart, whatever house it dwells within, can take on that electrified, exciting, eccentric, and potentially either chaotic or brilliant edge.

Challenge: Uranus can bring a sense of wired urgency and a craving for change, no matter the consequences. Its energy is nonlinear and can be chaotic and primordial, tense and nervous. When Uranus speaks to your chart and says it's time to transform the situation, go with it, because the more you resist inevitable change, the more Uranus shakes you up. On a tough day, Uranus can bring a destructive restless tendency to toss out the old just for the sake of change.

Practical: Uranus in your chart, the planets that it touches, and the house it inhabits point to where the lightning can strike in your chart. Here lie unexpected events that can be both brilliant and scary, and where you can take an ingenious and radical approach. Think of Uranus as the cosmic clutch that can help you change gears. This planet was discovered during the Industrial Revolution and signifies technology and change that tech brings. It signals electrical energy and the counterpart within your body and your nervous system. The Uranus in your chart shows where you want ingenuity and iconoclasts. It influences how you engage technology, the Internet, astrology, psychology, and political revolution, all things which can precipitate change.

Gift: Make good trouble. Sometimes what is stable and solid needs to be deconstructed in order to evolve into a new form. Uranus symbolizes that primordial wild energy, the unharnessed potential from which all new life springs. Uranus describes where you are willing to experiment or be spontaneous and open for a stroke of divine genius. It can help you be willing to release what is and search for what could be.

Affirmation: "Out of chaos can come crisis with opportunity; the unexpected can break the boundaries, crack us open, and electrify our future."

Uranus through the Signs

Uranus in Mars-ruled Aries adds extra lightning and more voltage to the nervous system, which can take you into brilliance, charisma, or craziness, depending upon what other planets it relates with and how you use the energy. The people of this generation can handle a crisis and are ready to change their world abruptly, but they must choose to add the forethought and goal to create constructive change instead of generalized chaos.

Uranus in Venus-ruled Taurus can feel paradoxical and add an ability to evolve the life and the world around us with stable change rather than shock it with a revolution. Or it could bring an earthquake—a personality that wants to consistently shake up the material world around us, changing borders and boundaries.

Uranus in Mercury-ruled Gemini could be taken for a lightweight, but don't be fooled. The Uranus-in-Gemini generation can be high-strung, full of crazy talk, or they can bring a revolution through their words and find a way to change the concepts in their field. Bring consciousness to the words and magic happens.

Uranus in Moon-ruled Cancer can bring change to the home front. This generation can work in politics to evolve their country or develop strange nationalistic edges. You may be unusually at home in technology and have an emotional connection to its equipment or the change it can bring. You could also rebel from traditional concepts of family and evolve a healthier version or renovate homes or ways of living.

Uranus in Sun-ruled Leo brings a strong personality and transformative persona. You may deal with an approach-avoidance conflict style about developing an identity in the world; you're torn between ambiguity and longing to be seen and to matter. This generation can use their very being or personality to create a platform for change. How that turns out depends on your intention: Are you working to grab an audience, or are you shining for all sentient beings?

Uranus in Mercury-ruled Virgo brings constant thoughtful improvement, a revolution of layers. This generation is deeply aware of what's wrong and what needs to be fixed in the world. You can work on that change piece by piece with your perceptive eyes and critical voice. If you develop a self-conscious edge, be kind to yourself in that personal evolution. All those pieces can add up to substantial transformation.

Uranus in Venus-ruled Libra considers dynamic balance. You can lean completely out of balance if your concept of the world is only fair to one side. Or you can bring us back into balance with a gift of fairness and social equity and through your transforming understanding of relationships. **Uranus in Mars and Pluto-ruled Scorpio** adds an undertone of insatiable curiosity. This generation wonders *what if.* They have a curiosity that can mischievously undermine or knock things over like a cat does just to see what happens or can ask the right questions and get down to the roots. This Uranus adds charismatic or complicated primal attraction and a personality that may be fascinated by extremes. **Uranus in Jupiter-ruled Sagittarius** adds mischief. This generation can enjoy saying what no one else is willing to say. But it's up to you to decide: Do you want to speak a shallow truth or look for deeper truths that can change the world? You could be called to find your version of the truth versus one you've been raised in and help this generation straighten out global misconceptions.

Uranus in Saturn-ruled Capricorn adds an electrical determination. This generation wants to break molds and climb higher, to change the rules with their steps forward. If you don't feel the top of the mountain is accessible, you can become determined to cause trouble. You see what needs to be done, so plug that electrical determination in to improving your lot and improve the world around you. We need you.

Uranus in Saturn and Uranus-ruled Aquarius challenges the molds and forms we live within. This generation can either swallow the rulebook and hold on to the theory of society they believe in or challenge every rule in the book and not so much lead a revolution as live a revolution. They live comfortably with their eccentricity in a way that challenges the people around them to rethink their own forms and process.

Uranus in Jupiter and Neptune-ruled Pisces adds an undertone of the transformative power of belief, fantasy, and sacrifice (whether that is your sacrifice, the belief that another person should sacrifice themselves or what they believe, or a sense of relinquishment and offering). Uranus in Pisces challenges you to, instead of sacrifice, share yourself and work through your obstacles as an offering. It also calls for a compassionate revolution; you may feel drawn to work for the benefit of all those who are vulnerable.

Neptune: Vision

Does your life feel too humdrum and mundane, hemmed in by concrete reality while you long for spiritual connection? Come swim with Neptune. Conversely, if you swim too deep in those waters of the collective unconscious and lose your way back to shore, ask for Neptune's direction. In your meditation, imagine that you are merging with Spirit, intuitively reading Spirit; feel your edges dissolve. Seek guidance in your dreams and imagination to align your life Spirit. Work with Neptune to find a healthy way to feed that hunger for Spirit, magic, and connection.

Neptune takes us into the realm of dreams, to the ocean of the collective unconscious, and draws metaphorical symbols from water. Think of the soft seep of spring rains in the wetlands and the overwhelming storms on the ocean. Neptune can create a portal into our intuition, imagination, and spirituality. Neptune is the modern co-ruler of Pisces and is in detriment in Virgo. The planet Neptune takes nearly 165 years around the zodiac, about 13 years in a sign, so it describes a generation, what they find beautiful, their spiritual and religious approach, how they seek reality versus fantasy.

Challenge: With Neptune we can get lost in the fog, long to escape, or mistake our imagination for reality. We can long for Spirit so much, we will take spirits, drugs, or alcohol to escape our gritty consensual reality, when what we are actually hungry for is magic and connection to the One. Where we have Neptune, it can be a challenge to be realistic, and we can become passive and feel martyred. Neptune also invokes a bendable reality, a place where we are tempted to lie and distort the truth or can be easily bamboozled by another's distortion. Neptune can lead us into all things foggy: misunderstandings, confusion, illusion, delusion, escapism, addiction, drowning, poisoning. We have to choose to pierce the fog and see the soul truth within.

Practical: When we are feeling awash, it can help to take a long bath and meditate to engage the positive side of Neptune. Neptune can also quite pragmatically deal with water, liquid, oils, leaks, floods things that flow, and all matters of the sea and seafaring. When it is not concretely dealing with liquids, this is a place that needs a creative and imaginative approach—then back that up with hard work and details. Neptune can also signify work with imagination, fiction, intuition, or the spiritual process.

Gift: Activate Neptune's gift by tapping into your intuition, your spiritual practice, and by applying your imagination. Neptune creates a portal into other realms, a way for Spirit to enter our life, a place for intuition and magic. It is a place where we work on subtle levels and can learn to trust our intuition. Neptune can help you remember that it is an illusion to believe we are separate from Spirit.

Affirmation: "With Neptune's help, through my spirit, through my imagination, through my dreams, I can transcend limitations and envision a better world. I am one with the One."

Neptune through the Signs

Neptune in Mars-ruled Aries can take an activist's approach to the spiritual search. This generation can seek a more militant view of life. Even in their deepest spiritual process, they tend to work with spiritual discipline and believe our vision should inform our actions.

Neptune in Venus-ruled Taurus adds an earthiness to the spirituality, which can idealize stuff and look for answers in management of money and resources. This generation see the sacred in our material world.

Neptune in Mercury-ruled Gemini can add a mesmerizing power to words, engaging in charismatic communication—for better or worse. Or it can loan a tendency to get lost by dispersing concentration, keeping too many plates spinning in the air.

Neptune in Moon- ruled Cancer can bring contact with that with the dream world and imagination. For some dwell in the spiritual path of nurturing and caring, others in the idealization of home and homeland, and others in the rich inner river of imagination.

Neptune in Sun-ruled Leo adds charisma, sunshine, and the complexities of ego. This generation can shine, and offer their light and hearth fire as a gift to the community. But they can also wrestle with feeling endangered by being visible or feel addicted to attention.

Neptune in Mercury-ruled Virgo will be subtle, not obvious in its effect; it empowers the person with the superpower of understanding the complexity of the situation. This generation can deal with painful doubt because they do not see things simply in black and white, but they bring this subtle brocaded understanding, this truer vision, to whatever they do.

Neptune in Venus-ruled Libra brings relational magic. This generation may need help finding the divine through their inner search but can see the divine in other people. This can bring an addiction to relationship or difficulty in seeing one another clearly, but they can also choose relationship to their muse, their guides, or to a balanced way of life. **Neptune in Mars- and Pluto-ruled Scorpio** can get addicted to extremes. But they can take us on a healing journey down to the depths and back again. Their spiritual approach can be transformative and intense. Even the nonbelievers can be fanatical about their nonbelief.

Neptune in Jupiter-ruled Sagittarius may take a more immediate experiential approach to their philosophy and may have to choose to look deep rather than operate on a philosophic assumption. They are drawn to an eclectic worldview or nature-based spiritual approach need room to roam in their mind body and soul.

Neptune in Saturn-ruled Capricorn adds seriousness to their spiritual path. They may need to work through some spiritual depressions. They want their philosophy to make sense to them. This generation can revive traditions or make new ones of their own, systems and disciplines that support their connection to the numinous.

Neptune in Saturn- and Uranus-ruled Aquarius as an eclectic philosophic edge. This generation may not want to be seen as religious or spiritual, or alternatively take on without question the complete package of a religious tradition. They may both be addicted to, or totally block, public opinion. Whatever path they take, they want their personal philosophy to make sense of it.

Neptune in Jupiter- and Neptune-ruled Pisces can get lost in Neptunian fantasy and want to believe their chosen reality rather than investigate a grittier shared reality. But if they choose to refine their perception instead of getting lost in the fantasy, this Neptune increases the ability to blend with other dimensions and be open to Spirit.

Pluto: Rebirth

If you're feeling disempowered, have dealt with loss or the misuse of power, or are facing some dark and difficult times, Pluto and Persephone can lend you strength and wisdom to change the dynamics and give it purpose. If you feel stuck in a dark place, ask Pluto to help you find the gold and jewels underneath this ground, understand the work you need to do down here, and find your way back with your spiritual gold when the work here is done.

Pluto speaks of the use and abuse of power, electrical power, political power, and personal empowerment. It symbolizes death and rebirth, any profound transformation, and speaks of your relationship to death and beyond. Pluto asks you to step up and be empowered, and to use that power within for the good of all.

Pluto takes about 248 years around the zodiac and is the modern ruler of Scorpio. It operates on a different plane than the rest of our solar system. It is the closest body of the Kuiper belt made of thousands of planetoids and particles that ring our solar system. Pluto acts as a doorway to the larger galactic realms. It is often a symbol of death and rebirth, down and back again, and can trigger some transformative journey that tests us mightily, shakes out our priorities, and brings us to a greater potential.

Challenge: Pluto plays hardball. Pluto can symbolize where you might be the victim of, or the perpetrator of, the misuse of personal, political, or electrical power, or point to the shadow world of backdoor politics and the criminal subculture. Pluto can point to a place where you feel powerless or out of control and are challenged to find the power within to turn your situation around. It can be a place where you brush mortality, where in your life are you faced with life-and-death questions and need to remember what is important.

Where you have Pluto, you can obsess, fixate, or become compulsive unless you work to heal the deep roots of your situation—and those roots may be in another life. These plutonic karmic boomerangs now need to be worked through with integrity. Don't try to make sense in this corner of your life, because the origins of these problems may be in another time and place, but do work a way forward that is best both you and all involved.

Practical: Pluto symbolizes the literal underworld of basements, plumbing, foundations. Pluto can also speak of what we dig up from under the ground, mining substances of worth, both pragmatically from the ground, like gold and jewels, and symbolically from the depths of your psyche, your personal unconscious, and the collective unconscious of the dream world.

Gift: Pluto asks, in the face of life and death, why are you here—and this is not a rhetorical question. Pluto wants you to have a good answer or be willing to search for one. Personal evolution is a good reason. With Pluto, you grow through making it through a hard time, through a descent to the underworld and your empowered return. Inanna, Persephone, Osiris, and all deities who descended to the underworld and returned as an empowered, compassionate God exemplify a potential Pluto journey. The best times in people's lives are often right after Pluto transits, as if they have distilled their understanding and focused their purpose, gained personal power, and burned through some difficult karma and are now ready to expand. A natal Pluto can feel like an intensely karmic point where the other world comes into your life.

As Pluto has been around the zodiac only once since the American Revolution, we don't have that much observed experience to go on, but the evidence is powerful.

Affirmation: *"In the face of life and death, I have purpose. I am willing to let go of old forms and beings to transform and bring in new life. I am willing to dig down deep, bring the dirt to the surface, sift out the dirt, and bring forth the hidden gold and jewels."*

Pluto through the Signs

Pluto in Mars-ruled Aries can believe in and be transformed by the power of heroism, war, and exploration.

Pluto in Venus-ruled Taurus can believe in and be transformed by the power of grounding and solidity.

Pluto in Mercury-ruled Gemini can believe in and be transformed by the power of exchanging ideas and expanding boundaries.

Pluto in Moon-ruled Cancer can believe in and be transformed by defining and protecting the power of home and homeland.

Pluto in Sun-ruled Leo can believe in and be transformed by the power of personality and self-expression. Can that personal exploration mature and empower?

Pluto in Mercury-ruled Virgo can believe in and be transformed by the power of analysis, analyzing oneself and the world, becoming aware of what the problem is and what needs to be done.

Pluto in Venus-ruled Libra can believe in and be transformed by the creative power of love, the arts, and questions of social justice.

Pluto in Mars and Pluto-ruled Scorpio can believe in and be transformed by looking at life and death straight in the eye, facing worst fears, and choosing life.

Pluto in Jupiter-ruled Sagittarius can believe in and be transformed by an awareness of their global citizenship, and by the interconnectedness of this world, its ecosystems, its politics, and its philosophies.

Pluto in Saturn-ruled Capricorn can believe in and be transformed by the power of organizations and authority through questioning what is our responsibility and how do we best inhabit it.

Pluto in Saturn and Uranus-ruled Aquarius can believe in and be transformed by the power of the people, the voice of the collective in all its horror and glory, and questions on how to balance individuality with the group needs.

Pluto in Jupiter and Neptune-ruled Pisces can believe in and be transformed by the power of individual surrender, sacrifice, and imagination.

RETROGRADE PLANETS

If you observe the planets from the Sun, all the planets orbit in the same direction and none ever appear to back up. But from our perspective here on Earth, because of the difference between our orbit and theirs, all the planets (except for the Sun and Moon) occasionally appear to stand still and then dance backward against the backdrop of the zodiac, as if the planet is doing a bunny hop, two steps forward and one step back. One way of thinking about it is to remember a subway or train ride where you were in a faster train passing a slower one—for a moment there you may get a disorienting feeling as the other train appears to back up—turn retrograde. Once you pull ahead, you can see that train is still moving forward, if not as fast as you.

When a planet retrogrades, events symbolized by that planet won't go as they normally do. Sometimes those activities get truly wonky. But for the most part a retrograde planet signals you to review, fix gaps, reconsider, and consolidate what you've learned in the last cycle before proceeding into the next chapter, as if you've been stopped before you head out on a trip and asked if you've remembered your toothbrush and turned off the stove. Many planets often retrograde in the northern summer and make it a perfect time to take time off, review our progress, catch up with ourselves, and reconnect with favorite people and places.

A retrograde planet in your natal chart suggests that part of your life may work differently than other people's. It could have some unique gifts and oddities that you need to explore for yourself rather than try to do it the way other people do. You could have walked into this life with some important skills, memories, or unfinished business in the areas symbolized by that planet, as if you are halfway through a project and have the groundwork done. But pay attention so you don't get hooked into less constructive old patterns to fulfill your unique potential.

Mercury retrograde is the most familiar of the retrograde cycles. Because the orbit of Mercury around the Sun is so fast—it orbits around the Sun in approximately 88 Earth days—Mercury appears retrograde to us Earthlings for approximately three weeks, three times a year. Mercury is the planet of movement and communication, all part of our daily activity, so this retrograde has a noticeable and tangible effect on our life. Ordinary communication, transportation, ideas, appointments, and reservations need to be handled with extra attention. Mercury can act as a trickster. All things mercurial can develop strange poltergeist; communication may snarl, traveling complicates, items wander, and misunderstandings can proliferate. An astrological adage points out that anything that begins reworks in a retrograde cycle, so it is time to reconsider, review, revisit, remember, and reconnect. Mercury retrograde can be a real gift that encourages us to take a break or dig things up from the past; tend to business long overdue and let the heart remember.

CHAPTER 5

YOUR INNER LANDSCAPE: CARDINAL POINTS AND HOUSES

The Sun is always moving forward, and all the planets in our solar system rotate both around and with the Sun as it revolves around the galactic center. It's a busy system. We'll get you oriented on this magical circle and then populate it with those characters.

We take a snapshot of all these planets and asteroids spinning around the Sun and note their relationship at the time and place of your first breath. If you don't have an accurate birth time, you can still get a great amount of information through the characters of the planets, their signs, and their relationships to one another, though you will miss a layer of information from the landscape those moving pieces inhabit.

ASTROLOGICAL POINTS

Venus Star point: Venus and the Sun conjunct roughly every nine months. The conjunction of Venus and the Sun before you were born resonates in your chart as a reflection of Venus and gives you clues about how you love, what draws you to another person, how you blend your Sun and Venus, your ego and your heart. In its circle around the stars, the Sun and Venus conjunct in a grouping of five signs, slowly circulating through the zodiac. Those five signs form a pentacle in the sky and reflect off each other in a helpful and healing dynamic. The Venus Star point is a relatively new study in astrology, and it is well worth investigating. If you pull your chart off the Internet and the Venus Star point is not there, you can do an Internet search for "calculate your Venus Star point" to find where yours resides.

Part of Fortune/Part of Spirit: Before there were computers, before we could see very far out into the sky, astrologers were using points they constructed with mathematical calculations based on the relationship between the Sun, Moon, and the ascendant. Nowadays the computer can find them for you.

The ones you'll see in your chart most often will be the Part of Fortune, which can act like a little Jupiter in your chart; it points to what can help you spot your resources and luck. The Part of Spirit points to your interior resources. There are different ways of arriving at these points, and, gratefully, computers do this for us these days, but it's good to know what we're seeing. These points marry each other and reverse between daytime and nighttime charts.

Part of Fortune in a day chart: Ascendant + Moon – Sun. In a night chart: Ascendant – Moon + Sun.

The Part of Spirit in a day chart: Ascendant - Moon + Sun. In a night chart: Ascendant + Moon – Sun.

THE ASCENDANT OR RISING SIGN: ENTRANCE

Like the front door of a house, the ascendant is the entrance to the landscape of your chart; it is how you see the world and how the world sees you.

When you look at the circle of your chart, put yourself in the center. This is your place of birth. From here, imagine pointing to the eastern horizon, where the Sun would be at sunrise. The degree of the zodiac just rising at that moment of your birth is your rising sign or ascendant.

The line that bisects the circle underneath your feet, from east to west, from ascendant to descendant, represents the surface of the Earth. The circle doesn't describe the Earth but a sphere projected out from you at your point of birth. The bottom half of the circle is beneath the Earth; the top half describes the bowl of the sky.

The cardinal points work like the points on the compass and orient us. Here we look at the eastern horizon, the western horizon, and directly above you and below you. You can think of these as tent poles or electric conductors that connect you to your world.

Ascendant: As you imagine standing there in the middle of the circle, point to the left side, the east, your rising sign. This symbolizes your front door, your first impression that greets people when you first walk in the room, your interface system. The planet that rules the sign on your ascendant plays a key role in how you interact with the world.

IC: Draw a line through you, down your spine, through the center of the Earth, and out the other side, and you locate your IC, or Imum Coeli, which translates from Latin as the "bottom of the sky." This is the taproot of the chart and is the cusp, or the doorway, of the fourth house, a point that describes your roots, your foundation, and all that feeds you from your lineage.

Descendant: Look to the right of the chart, to the western point, where the Sun will descend at sunset, and see the descendant, the aperture where other people walk into your life. This is the cusp of the seventh house, home of your equal partnerships with people you work with, love, argue with, and marry.

MH: Draw a line from the center of the Earth, up through you and into the heavens, and come to the MH, the midheaven, the flagpole on top of your building, your most public self, your professional interface, how you broadcast to the world. This is the cusp of your tenth house, the house of profession, authority, and public visibility.

Notice that the east and the west are the opposite to what you would see on a regular road map. This is because you are inside this map looking out. The chart is not about how outsiders see you, not your convenient external self, but a map of your internal being from your inner perspective out. Work with this metaphor.

The ascendant describes how you enter the world, and action in the houses on this half of the chart originates from you. The descendant describes how others enter your life, and the action in houses on this half of the chart originate in your interaction with others, family, loves, work, and others' ideas and resources.

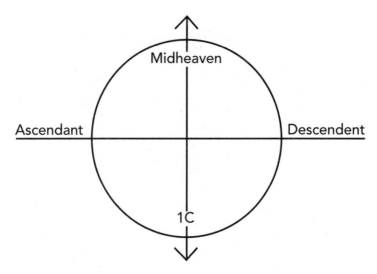

Those bisecting lines quarter the chart, and each quadrant has its own weight.

Astrologers then divide each of those quadrants up into three houses to get another layer of information.

The Earth rotates completely around its axis within 24 hours, so the mandala of this chart rotates through the zodiac completely in approximately 24 hours. A new sign shows up on the ascendant roughly every two hours. There are 30 degrees to each sign, so a new degree rises roughly every four minutes. You can think of the degrees like an address number on a block: They help you know the cross street and find the place. The border of each house, called the cusp, is the doorway or entrance into that house.

Now let's take a look at a few charts of notable individuals to understand how everything weaves together to create a stellar landscape.

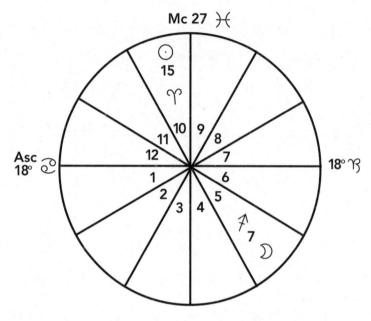

Ram Dass was born close to noon with the Sun at the top of the chart in Aries, in the visible and authoritative tenth house. His chart was built on this Aries foundation. He was trailblazer of philosophy and spirituality, a rebel of consciousness. His Sagittarius Moon denotes his ebullient spirit and his sense that he was a global citizen, a being known for his openness, honesty, and forthrightness. The entrance to his chart, his rising sign, is in Cancer, the sign of cultural caretaker or parent, an empathetic counterbalance to his fire Sun and Moon, which made him approachable. That's what people first read when they met him.

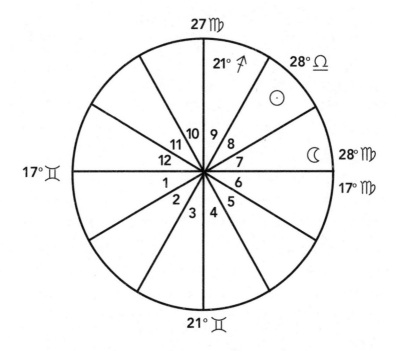

Deepak Chopra, this intelligent seeker and healer, has a chart with his Sun in kindly, balanced Libra, in the investigative, curious eighth house, and his Moon, his emotional prime directive, in the reserved, intellectual, and potentially healing-oriented sign of Virgo, who wants to understand how the details fit together into a healthy whole. The entrance to this chart is a soft-spoken, empathic Pisces ascendant.

Take a look at your chart and note the signs and houses of your Sun, Moon, and rising sign. Then, create a story about it. Your sun sign and place maps your energy source, your Moon sign and place, an emotional prime directive, and your rising sign, what people first meet when you walk in the door.

THE HOUSES: YOUR INNER VILLAGE

On top of the framework of the cardinal points, we sketch in a village around the town square, and each house in that village describes a compartment or stage setting in your life.

When you look at your chart, imagine you're looking at the map of a village, your interior town, with you standing in the center of the village square. Take the roof off all the houses around the village square and see who is in which house. Notice who populates this inner village—the archetypal characters of the planets, asteroids, and nodes. Who's in the bank (second house, your resources), the temple or hospital (twelfth house, your inner psyche and long-term health, and any organization large enough to feel like a hive), the elementary school (third house), college (ninth), etc. We'll come back and walk through each house.

The cusp of each house, the degree of the sign on its leading edge, is the doorway into that room. Look to the planet that rules that sign. Check out its place, gifts, and troubles for more information about how you relate to that compartment.

Next we'll talk about how these planets relate through aspects, through resonance by mode and element.

Remember in this map that you, or the subject of the chart, are inside the circle looking out, so the east is on the left and the west is on the right of the circle. If you were inside a clock looking out, the numbers would appear to go counterclockwise or widdershins around the circle, and so would the astrological houses. Remember this is from your perspective, not the perspective of someone else looking into your personal experience.

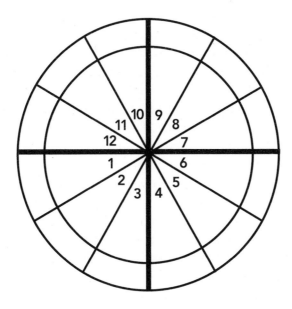

Astrologers use many different house systems. After 40-plus years of experimentation, I use the Koch house system. Most modern Western systems of houses (and there are many—see the glossary) use the same ascendant, descendant, IC, and midheaven but divide the rest of the houses up using different systems. You can think of the cardinal points as the load-bearing walls of a house and the interstitial house cusps as movable, semipermeable walls. In my experience you really notice the difference when a planet crosses the cardinal points, like the moment right before sunrise (Sun in the first house) and right after (Sun in the twelfth). Equal sign-house systems place those cardinal points within the signs rather than using them as a house cusp. Traditional whole-sign houses are seeing a resurgence in popularity. It takes the sign on the ascendant as the whole first house and gives a house to each sign thereafter. The system is useful for seeing patterns but, to some astrologers, misses a level of information. Again, there is no wrong system in astrology, just different ways of slicing the orange. Try a few house systems on and see what works for you.

As you put these patterns together, you can think of this process like playing the game Clue—think of Colonel Mustard, in the library, with a candlestick, for example. With astrology, it's something like Mars, in Capricorn, in the third house, with a trine to Uranus. That energetic Mars archetype suggests the ability for determined, impassioned communication (because of the third-house placement) developed by supportive but challenging rivalry (Mars exalted in Capricorn with an empowering trine to electrifying Uranus) with strong-willed siblings, classmates, or neighbors (the third house talks about communication we developed in our early life and how we communicate within our local community). If this was your chart, it would be up to you whether you use that determination to be a contentious bully, a determined engineer, or a hero and advocate for those with less of a voice, all possible outcomes from that configuration.

Here you are beginning to understand the mandala map of your chart, that interwoven quilt created through the interaction of all the planets, signs, houses, and aspects.

THE 12 ASTROLOGICAL HOUSES

Here in the West we divide the chart into 12 sections or houses numbered 1 through 12, counterclockwise, starting with the ascendant, and allow each of those sections to refer to a compartment of our life.

The houses go around in a circle and form a mandala. You can spiral through this on many levels, and all these levels fit together and influence one another. Eventually these layers can create a hologram in your mind of meaning and interrelationship. The first round can be the compartments of your life, from how you enter the world—first house—through your relationships, your work, to the twelfth house of who you are in quiet and private.

Because our psyche is built over time, the chart can also be read as the stages of life that formed us. The first house has a relationship to our infancy, the fifth house to our early romance, the seventh to growing partnership, the tenth to our career peak, and the twelfth to our elder introspection.

Around once more you can look at the parts of your body. The first house relates to the head down to the twelfth house, which relates to the feet.

First notice the sign on the cusp and where the ruler of that sign dwells, which is particularly important and telling for empty houses. Then notice who lives in that house, what planets, asteroids, and points dwell there.

Look at your chart and notice your busy houses—that is, houses with two or more planets within—to get an overall impression of your spirit village. When you have a busy house, ponder if this house, and the one opposite, which may need to be developed to balance your life, are full of events, issues, and growth opportunities.

Now, let's go through each house in depth.

First House: Arrival

The cusp of the first house is the ascendant, or rising sign. Planets here are just about to rise over the eastern horizon. In your village the first house would be the welcome center and information bureau at the entrance.

Challenge: You are responsible for how the world sees you and how you see the world. If you feel like people get the wrong impression of you, look here for clues about how you project yourself. If you project leadership, say, with an Aries rising, but don't want to lead with integrity, people will lose trust. Hide behind a nondescript persona and people may never know how wonderful you are. If you don't like how you are perceived, exercise the gift of your rising sign and its ruling planet.

Conversely, your rising sign is a two-way window and speaks about the filters through which you perceive your world. Do you filter through an experience of privilege or control, through sharp edges and defense, to sexual attraction, or do you filter new information in through your preconceptions?

Practical: This is your information bureau; here you can help people understand you and make people feel welcome, comfortable, and intrigued in your presence. Understand the first impressions you make, as well as the hints to become more comfortable in your interactions, to help you make a grand entrance or be invisible as needed. Look to the first and twelfth houses for information about how you were born and how you walk into any new situation.

Gift: You can't walk away from your filters, but the more you understand how the world sees you and through which filters you see the world, the more clearly and transparent these perceptions can become. Take responsibility for your public persona; it could be radically different than your private persona, but the two need to work together.

To learn more about your first house, consider the following questions:

Who is in your first house?

What sign is on the cusp, the doorway to the first house?

What planet is the ruler of that sign?

Which house does that planet call home?

This tells a story about your relationship to how you enter the world, how you see the world, and how the world sees you. What potential challenges, lessons, and gifts do you see in this house and through its ruler?

Second House: Resources

In your inner village, this house could be your bank or storehouse. The second house symbolizes your relationship to the material world, your attitude toward money, your stuff, and your body—which was your first resource. It also speaks about what you care enough about—to grow and invest in—to make money. The symbolism starts in that phase of your childhood when you are first exploring this material world, crawling around and getting to know how this body works.

Challenge: There may be ambiguity about material things; any love-hate relationships or mixed messages to the world about income and possessions show here. We can see what you crave and where you put your material security. Look to this house, its contents, and its rulers to straighten out your attitude and message about your goods and services so the world can respond back to you with clarity.

Practical: What you value enough to make money with, your attitude toward money, goods, and embodiment.

Gift: Your body is your temple. This house speaks of the sacred earthen vessel for your spirit, for all your good works, your body. You can give generously with what you value and be a resource for others when you feel right with your world.

To learn more about your second house, consider the following questions:

Who is in your second house?

What sign is on the cusp, the doorway to the second house?

What planet is the ruler of that sign?

Which house does that planet call home?

Tell a story about your relationship to how you enter the world, how you see the world, and how the world sees you. What potential challenges, lessons, and gifts do you see in this house and through its ruler?

Third House: Communication

In your inner village the third house could be the schoolhouse, the local radio station, and the coffeehouse where you meet neighbors and post your notices. It signifies your siblings and sibling-like friends, your early educational experiences, and how you learned to communicate in those early years.

Challenge: Trauma from your early schooling or problems with siblings, sibling-like friends, or neighbors show up here. How you were trained to communicate has a long-term effect on your mental muscles and how your mind works.

Practical: The third house can give you solid tools to deal with your siblings and sibling-like relationships. It can sketch out how you learn, how you felt about school, and how you have learned to speak, write, and communicate. This pattern echoes how you feel about driving, commuting, and how you relate to your neighborhood.

Gift: Come to know your mind and how your thinking was constructed. The third house can give you clues to your best meditation techniques to still and clear the mind. It offers a map to clarify your communication and speak the truth from your heart.

To learn more about your third house, consider the following questions:

Who is in your third house?

What sign is on the cusp, the doorway to the third house?

What planet is the ruler of that sign? Which house does that planet call home?

Tell a story about your relationship to your sibling and sibling-like relationships, your relationship to your neighborhood, and how you communicate. Write about your journey with your third house. What potential challenges, lessons, and gifts do you see in this house and through its ruler?

Fourth House: Home

In your inner village, this is your home base. It speaks about your relationship to the parent whose job it was to nurture you and to the family that gave you roots. It describes what meant home to you as a child and how you feel about your own home and sanctuary in the future.

Challenge: This houses the effects that your early home life and family dynamics may have had on you. If warm and healthy, these are patterns you will want to bring into the future. However, if it was toxic or traumatic, it may present future challenges. Here you have to do your inner homework to clear the memory and the family bloodlines. If ghosts from the past weigh on your present life, clear unwanted baggage of all types out of your psychic basement.

To illustrate the challenges that come with the fourth house, take the examples of three of my clients. All three had the difficult planets Pluto, Mars, and Uranus, all in the fourth house of home. I described the qualities of tense, unsettled, martial energy with challenging power dynamics to them. It turns out that the first client had had a truly traumatic childhood and was still wounded and embittered but getting therapy. The second also had a traumatic childhood but had mentors and had recovered and become a truly skilled social worker who worked with families in trauma, and they loved that work. The third one said no, he'd had a lovely childhood, but his father was a general, and they moved between military bases and sometimes had bombs in the basement. Each was expressing the same symbols with different patterns.

Practical: Your taproot, your early home life, and your sense of home and homeland based on that early time. Look here for information about how you were nurtured and fed and what you inherited—for better or worse—from the nurturers in your family. This house can be quite literal: the house you live in and its foundations and basement and all things that come out of the ground. It's what feels cozy and familiar to you. This house describes what helps you feel at home now and how you bring things to conclusion.

Gift: Your deepest psyche, your dearest home, your place of sanctuary, this house offers hints as to how to clear and reclaim your home and sense of family and chosen family. Create sanctuary within and without and renew.

To learn more about your fourth house, consider the following questions:

Who is in your fourth house?

What sign is on the cusp, the doorway to the fourth house?

What planet is the ruler of that sign? Which house does that planet call home?

Tell a story about your relationship to your early home, your roots, what helps you feel at home now. Write about your journey with your fourth house. What potential challenges, lessons, and gifts do you see in this house and through its ruler?

Fifth House: Passion

The fifth house is your art studio and performance space or the club where you meet exciting people and show off your skills in your inner village. It's a place to take your date in those early stages of romance, and a place to take your children for a wonderful outing. It is where your adolescent self lives and expresses, where you can find that creative spark and joy. Look here for clues about your love expressed to the world in the form of children, creative process, and the luminescent liminal stage of love affairs.

Challenge: As this house talks about your inner adolescent, it is not a place of maturity. It speaks of that hot-pink swirling storm of a love affair or creative fit, the addiction to love and drama, and the adrenaline rush around risk and gambling. It can map out trouble with children as well as creative blocks and can give us clues on how to break through those blocks.

Practical: This house is connected to the heart and chest, to your heart given to the world in the form of entertainment, romance, love affairs, children, and the products and process of creativity, books, paintings, dance, and performance. Here life can be a party.

Gift: This house can describe your relationship to your artistic muse. When other houses are supported, it can help keep the spark of romance alive within partnership, and help keep that creative spark alive in your work and art forms. Here you can heal relationships between generations through shared joyful experiences. When a heart is on fire from the vagaries of love, it can help to express the fifth house in another way, to love others, share ourselves generously, paint our heart out, and dance our feelings to the sky.

To learn more about your fifth house, consider the following questions:

Who is in your fifth house?

What sign is on the cusp, the doorway to the fifth house?

What planet is the ruler of that sign?

Which house does that planet call home?

Tell a story about how you express your heart in the world—your creative process, relationship to children, and how you fall in love. Write about your journey with your fifth house. What potential challenges, lessons, and gifts do you see in this house and through its ruler?

Sixth House: Sustainability

In your inner village, the sixth house would be a workplace, health clinic, dog kennel, bathroom sink, and medicine cabinet. The sixth house relates to that phase of life when you realize you might need a job if you are going to have romance and take that inner teenager to a party. Do you take care of yourself? This house deals with your daily work, co-workers, and employees, not necessarily your calling and profession. It can describe your daily habits, how you deal with any short-term health issues, like a passing cold or indigestion, and what helps you stay healthy. It reflects your relationship to small animals, pets, and even houseplants.

Challenge: Here you see what could lead you to either overwork and exhaust yourself or have a block on doing regular work that will support your life. How you might somaticize your feelings rather than deal with them. How does your life or attitude contribute to sickness? If you have trouble at your workplace or between you and your co-workers, look here for clues to unconscious habits that contribute to the problem.

Practical: The sixth house gives you clues about your job, your sense of service. Notice how your relationship to your unconscious habits of self-care, or lack thereof, also can be mirrored in your relationship to your pets. The sixth house of daily work can support your tenth house of profession or calling.

Gift: How do you sweep your temple? Here you can find a map to create a sustainable ecology in your life, a life that feeds you as much or more than it takes from you. Map out what you need to create a healthier life. Notice what actually feeds you in your daily job, and grow those elements. Also consider how your relationship to your pets add life to your life.

To learn more about your sixth house, consider the following questions:

Who is in your sixth house?

What sign is on the cusp, the doorway to the sixth house?

What planet is the ruler of that sign? Which house does that planet call home?

Tell a story about how your practical habits and work life affect your health and how you related to your pets. What potential challenges, lessons, and gifts do you see in this house and through its ruler?

Seventh House: Relationship

In your inner village, the seventh house could be the restaurant where you meet for a romantic dinner or to confer with all your important equal others, your lawyer, spouse, business partner, or nemesis. This house is where the Sun would be during sunset, a most relatable and romantic time.

Challenge: This can be a place where you ask other people to hold some important part of your persona rather than live it out yourself, and as such hand over your power. It is important that you own the energy of all these planets. For example, if your Sun is in the seventh house, you may be drawn to strong personalities rather than choose to develop your own. When a part of you is externalized and being held by another, whether that is a business partner or a romantic companion, it can be used as blackmail to control you.

Practical: The seventh house shows how you let other equals into your life. It governs partnerships of all kinds—attitudes toward marriage and spouses, business partnerships, consultants, combatants, legal battles, and open warfare. It offers clues about who you are drawn to and how they enter your life.

Gift: Develop that quality you find love-worthy in another and then you can partner with it safely. Look to your seventh house for clues about your relationship training and assumptions. As you become more conscious of these patterns, you can partner your own soul, with spirit, and bring wonderful equal others into your life in a dynamic, equal way.

To learn more about your seventh house, consider the following questions:

Who is in your seventh house?

What sign is on the cusp, the doorway to the seventh house?

What planet is the ruler of that sign? Which house does that planet call home?

Tell a story about your relationship to all the equal others in your life, your partners of love and work, your counselors, and your open enemies. What potential challenges, lessons, and gifts do you see in this house and through its ruler?

Eighth House: Mystery

In your inner village, here you would find the loan office, the lawyer's office where the wills are kept, and behind those strange portals into the mysteries of life, death, and sexuality. Opposite to your second house of resources is how you relate to other people's resources and money, values, power, bodies, psychic thoughts, and stories.

Challenge: Sex, loans, and valuables can bring up so much guilt—and manipulation. In the eighth house you see how you were trained to deal with power dynamics. Look for clues around struggles in family inheritance, whether you inherited money, poverty, or emotional patterns, familial debt, neuroses, or obligations. In the symbolism involved, you can also see compulsive dynamics around your sexuality and sexual dynamics. It also speaks about how you relate to other people's thoughts, how you use this laser-like form of intuition. Here you can see how you pick up other people's thought forms or opinions and not know they're not yours until you develop more conscious boundaries.

Practical: Look to the eighth house for clues about how you can more consciously negotiate a loan, apply for a grant, or choose financial independence instead. How do you solve mysteries or develop a question-oriented psychic intuition, and how can you use divination tools like a Ouija board or tarot cards safely and productively? And here you can investigate one of the great personal mysteries and map what excites you and what repulses you around sex and all intimate relationships.

Gift: Develop that eighth-house curiosity, empower yourself to form your own value system, one that is good for you and all sentient beings. By consciously stepping out of power over dynamics and into empowerment for all, you can work to free your relationship to money, support, and the exchange of physical joy. The eighth house is where you can transcend ordinary reality, step forward into the unknown, and seek mystery, including the great mysteries, and explore how you are connected at your core.

To learn more about your eighth house, consider the following questions:

Who is in your eighth house?

What sign is on the cusp, the doorway to the eighth house? What planet is the ruler of that sign? Which house does that planet call home?

Tell a story about your relationship to other people's resources, sex, taxes, inheritance, and grants. How have the dynamics around death affected your life? What potential challenges, lessons, and gifts do you see in this house and through its ruler?

Ninth House: Exploration

In your inner village square, the ninth house would be the travel agency and international airport, the broadcast studio, the college and its library, the Internet café . . . All things that can expand your world.

Challenge: The ninth house describes how you look elsewhere for an answer. Do you look for a geographical cure and want to leave town rather than work through a problem? Do you imagine the grass is greener and the world more interesting on the other side of town or the other side of the globe? The ninth house can also point to a pattern of spiritual bypassing where you use your philosophy to unconsciously justify what you want so you can skip the messy work of introspection and interpersonal relationships. You can also find clues about how you might block yourself from becoming visible in the bigger world, through broadcast, publishing, or taking the risk of lifelong learning. If you feel curtailed and stuck, afraid or unable to grow your world, look to the ninth house for clues to travel beyond those bounds.

Practical: The ninth house maps how to expand your world. It can help you map the path to higher education, international understanding, broadcasting, publicity, philosophy, and metaphysics. It helps you understand how you like or don't like to travel outside of familiar territory and how you feel about foreign cultures, accents, world music, the rhythms of a global citizen. Look here for clues about getting your website up and getting publicity when you need it.

Gift: The ninth house opens your psyche and your mind to the philosophies and understandings of the world at large. Here you can map how you travel both in the body and in the psyche through shamanic journey. Look for clues here to travel through dreams and on the astral plane, expand your metaphysics, or be touched by spirituality and spiritual paths from faraway places.

To learn more about your ninth house, consider the following questions:

Who is in your ninth house?

What sign is on the cusp, the doorway to the ninth house?

What planet is the ruler of that sign?

Which house does that planet call home?

Tell a story about your relationship to how you explore and expand your world, and how you travel in mind, body, or spirit. What potential challenges, lessons, and gifts do you see in this house and through its ruler?

Tenth House: Authority

Around your village square, the tenth house would be the mayor's house, the CEO's office in the town's biggest business, the principal's office, the VIP box in the stadium, and a parent's favorite chair. It is the seat of authority within you and without. Your tenth house is modeled, for better or for worse, by your relationship to the parent figure you see as most connected to the world at large.

Challenge: Did you question authority, respect it, or learn to distrust it? Did you have to sneak around to become yourself? It's hard to step into a position of authority yourself if you do not have a good map or relationship to outside authority. Conversely, if you've never struggled with authority, you may not have compassion for those who really don't like it when you tell them what to do. If you couldn't trust your parents, it can be a challenge to trust Spirit. If the very nature of authority, yours or others, is a struggle for you, look here for the higher notes of each planet involved as a way to heal and transcend this relationship.

Practical: The Sun is here at noon, the most public time of the day. The tenth house is the flagpole on top of your soul's home, your route toward personal authority through your parents, mentors, and teachers. It can map your relationship to managers and bosses and how you can evolve into one yourself. Look here for information about your most public professional self, your career, and how you were trained to stand up, be responsible, and be seen in the world. If you didn't have good role models, go look for ones now; look for people who use their worldly power in a good way and investigate how you can step into that role with others.

Gift: Your relationship to the divine, however you experience it—the God or the Gods, the Creator/Creation, the Divine Parents—can take its map from your relationship to the authority structures you've come to know. Listen to the spiritual wisdom of that voice within and use it to be of service. Listen here for calls to be the hands of Spirit in this world.

To learn more about your tenth house, consider the following questions:

Who is in your tenth house?

What sign is on the cusp, the doorway to the tenth house?

What planet is the ruler of that sign?

Which house does that planet call home?

Tell a story about your relationship to authority—yours and others, your profession, and your relationship to the elements of your family that showed you how to go on in the world. Write about your journey with your tenth house. What potential challenges, lessons, and gifts do you see in this house and through its ruler?

Eleventh House: Community

In your inner village, the eleventh house is the corner of the park where you hang out with, or avoid, your peers as a teenager. This house holds your community center, town council, meeting chamber, and your friendship group.

Challenge: Do you care what other people think more than you value what *you* think? Do you care too much about what's going on in community, or, conversely, do you avoid the work of friendship? If meetings and the collaborative process drive you nuts or you have trouble socializing without feeling lost, look to the eleventh house for clues that will work for you.

Practical: Map your relationship to meetings, circles, local politics, unions, a book club, teamwork—all your collective experiences. Look here for clues about how to grow a friendly community and meet new people comfortably. Look for clues to what works for you in a meeting. Notice what characteristics draw you into a friendship and what you learn vicariously through your friendships, as you may be drawn to people with specific issues or problems for you to learn from without you having to go through those problems yourself.

Gift: Here you can create sangha, a spiritual community of like-minded people supporting one another on a path, whether that is a formal meditation group, devotees to spiritual practice, a distant online network, or informal friends who offer one another heart-centered support. Look for breadth as well as depth in your connections to make the most of this house; diverse points of view and skills can stretch you to grow and create strong and healthy teams.

To learn more about your eleventh house, consider the following questions:

Who is in your eleventh house?

What sign is on the cusp, the doorway to the eleventh house?

What planet is the ruler of that sign? Which house does that planet call home?

Tell a story about your relationship to community, teams, and your network of friends. What potential challenges, lessons, and gifts do you see in this house and through its ruler?

Twelfth House: Introspection

If this were your village square, the twelfth house is where you can be alone, whether it's that first hour after Sunrise for prayer, yoga, or deep sleep, or somewhere you go on personal retreat. It's that place in your mind where you can feel alone in a crowd, either as a refuge or in isolation, or the therapist's office where you do your deepest work. The planets in the twelfth house have just risen over the eastern horizon when you were born. They describe soul issues that could be the least visible to the outside world but that fill your inner realm. They can motivate you as an adult and push you into your deepest work.

Challenge: Until you become conscious of your motivations, they can echo in your health or be reflected at you by the world around you. Here your shadow boomerangs back toward you. For example, if you have Mars here and do not acknowledge your power or anger, then you may have to develop your inner warrior through fighting others' efforts to disempower you. The argument might be with your body; you may need to bargain with your immune system to work for you, not against you. Look to the sign on the cusp of the twelfth, its ruler and content, for a map of hidden forces from other lives and hidden patterns in the body and the psyche.

Practical: The planets in the twelfth house have just risen over the eastern horizon when you were born. They describe soul issues, which could be the least visible to the outside world but that fill your inner realm. The twelfth house reflects in your relationships to organizations that are so large (such as corporations, hospitals, prisons, monasteries, or ashrams), you might feel alone even in a crowd, like a bee in the hive. Is this a natural milieu for you, one that allows you to accomplish a lot without being in the spotlight, or do you feel lost in that crowd? It can map your deep inner world and traces of your last lives. Here you find clues about your long-term health, and how your mind and body reflect one another.

Gift: Look here to understand your inner world, your prayer life, and time in your temple. This house speaks of that form of intuition that acts like a sponge and soaks up your surroundings. Here you can explore and enrich your precious time alone and find your connection to your Source. You may find clues to your deepest karmic work.

To learn more about your twelfth house, answer the following questions:

Who is in your twelfth house?

What sign is on the cusp, the doorway to the twelfth house?

What planet is the ruler of that sign? Which house does that planet call home?

Tell a story about your relationship to your inner world. Investigate how your mind-body system affects your long-term health. How do you relate to the spirit realm and all organizations in your life that are big enough to feel like a beehive. What potential challenges, lessons, and gifts do you see in this house and through its ruler?

HOUSES IN PAIRS OF OPPOSITES

We can better understand the houses by comparing the relationship between one house and the house directly across the circle.

The first house describes how you enter the world. The house opposite it, **the seventh**, describes how others enter your world.

The second house describes your resources, while **the eighth** house represents how you relate to other people's resources, their thoughts, bodies, stuff, or money.

The third house refers to early education, how you learned to think and communicate through your early school experience, as well as your familiar neighborhood. **The ninth** house describes how you expand your world and go exploring.

The fourth house speaks of your early home life and how you create home, versus **the tenth house**, which explores your career and your relationship to authority and the public.

The fifth house speaks to how you shine and offer love to the world in the form of romance, children, and creative process. On the other hand, **the eleventh** house shares how you receive love and connection through collective experiences, community, and friendships.

The sixth house refers to your short-term health, workaday world, and daily habits. Opposite it, **the twelfth** house connects to your long-term health, inner world, and unconscious and superconscious reality.

DERIVED HOUSES

Farther on down the road, when you are ready to notice more layers of complicated information, you can work with derived houses. We derive the meaning of the houses by following the house pattern around and around in spirals to answer a question. For example, if the seventh house describes equal partners in your life, like your mate, then clues to your mate's money can be found in your eighth house, or the second house to the seventh. Clues to your mate's relationship to their mother and early upbringing can be found in your tenth (the fourth to the seventh). Clues to your mother-in-law's dog can be found in your third (the sixth to the tenth), and so on around the circle. Don't worry about this now; this is just a peek ahead. It's astounding how well the house system works. It points perfectly to the interrelationship of all the threads of our life.

CHAPTER 6

THE CONVERSATIONS: ASPECTS, PLANETARY CONTAINMENT, AND CHART PATTERNS

You've sketched out your inner village, you know who manages each of the houses, and you populated the houses of your village with your planets, asteroids, nodes, and other astrological points.

Now we'll map the conversation between them. What are your strength-building challenges? What are the flowing resources you have to work with?

Aspects are beams of energy that light up when the planets involved move into geometric patterns with one another.

They form lines of communication between the planets and describe their conversation. Supportive aspects build energy and a synergistic rapport; challenging aspects irritate, teach tough lessons, and build strength. When two or more planets have these relationships by aspects in your natal chart, they always resonate together. Like an autoharp cord where you press one button and three strings are touched, when any transiting planet hits one of these aspected planets, the other resonates with it; they develop a lifelong bond.

Like every other thing in astrology, each aspect represents a continuum, a challenging edge, a practical side, and a positive gift or resource we can draw from. It's easier to see the gifts on the sof,t supporting aspects, and it's easier to see the challenge on the hard aspects, but it's always up to you how you use these aspects. Be aware of the challenging aspect, be kind to yourself about it, and develop its positive gift. You can't pretend these aspects don't exist. If these planets were in conversation when you were born, they will resonate all your life, but you do get to choose how to direct that conversation.

You can find your aspects on your natal chart and the graph that usually comes with it. When you look at a chart drawn out from most websites, you'll see lines running between planets. Usually the charts are drawn using red or orange, warm colors for the challenging aspects, blue for the flowing aspects, and green for the thoughtfully irritating aspects. If you don't see them drawn out, you can look for an aspect grid that comes with most charts to see the relationship between any two planets; read one planet down, the other across.

We'll go through the nature of all the aspects, then talk about orb—how close they need to be to be in conversation. And then we'll walk through the phases of the Moon, which are formed by the conversation between the Sun and the Moon, as an example of how aspects have a cycle and wax and wane.

The aspects don't have to be exact to the degree; they just have to be within orb to feel it. If aspects are like beams of light between two planets, that light is strongest at the exact point, but it is still felt, if fading out, at the edges of the beam. The orb is the distance between planets that still feels that beam.

Let's use Sri Aurobindo's chart, on page 156, as an example.

Like building a sculpture, we start with the fundamental aspects and then flesh the chart out from there. Note the aspects first to the Sun and Moon. These are foreground and play a major role. Then check out the aspects to the planets in order of proximity to the Sun; start with Mercury, then Venus, Mars, Jupiter, Saturn, Uranus, Netune, and Pluto.

Look for major aspects first, as they are strongest aspects, in the foreground, and are the easiest to spot. We have been working with these major Ptolemaic aspects since Ptolemy introduced them back in the 1st century A.D. The minor aspects are more subtle; they divide our circle up into smaller sections and hit different residences. Each has its own flavor.

Grand trine: Sri Aurobindo, born in 1872 in India, was both a philosopher poet and a pragmatic journalist and Indian nationalist. He brought integral yoga to the Western world. Note the Sun and Jupiter close together, and with Jupiter the same degree, an exact conjunction to the ascendant. The Moon is in a freedom-loving, philosophical Sagittarius trine, the Sun and expansive Jupiter are in the first house, and both the Sun and the Moon trine Neptune, forming a grand trine in outreaching fire signs. These indicate am expansive thinker with a big personality, with Neptune in Aries in the ninth house of philosophy and faraway places. He used his personality (Sun-Jupiter-ascendant conjunction) to platform his liberating theology both at home and as an educator and philosopher abroad, with his Neptune in the ninth. Find the trines in his chart below, both in the circle, and on the grid. This grand trine is the dominant pattern in his chart. All the other aspects flesh out this picture.

Note the conjunction between Mars and Uranus. Although it is across sign with Mars in Cancer and Uranus in Leo, they are only five degrees apart, and Mars, the fast-moving planet, is approaching Uranus, so it is in applying aspect.

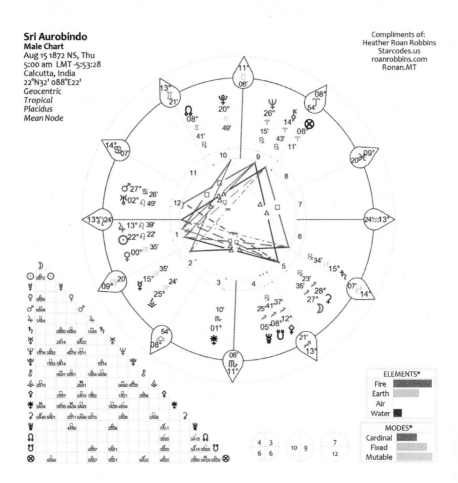

Sri Aurobindo
Male Chart
Aug 15 1872 NS, Thu
5:00 am LMT -5:53:28
Calcutta, India
22°N32' 088°E22'
Geocentric
Tropical
Placidus
Mean Node

Compliments of:
Heather Roan Robbins
Starcodes.us
roanrobbins.com
Ronan.MT

Asp	Name	Angle
☌	Conjunction	0°00'
☍	Opposition	180°00'
△	Trine	120°00'
□	Square	90°00'
✶	Sextile	60°00'
∠	Semisquare	45°00'
⚼	Sesquisquare	135°00'
⚻	Quincunx	150°00'

Sg	Name	Sg	Name
♈	Aries	♎	Libra
♉	Taurus	♏	Scorpio
♊	Gemini	♐	Sagittarius
♋	Cancer	♑	Capricorn
♌	Leo	♒	Aquarius
♍	Virgo	♓	Pisces

Pt	Name	Sg	Hs
☽	Moon	♐	5
☉	Sun	♌	1
☿	Mercury	♍	2
♀	Venus	♍	1
♂	Mars	♋	12
♃	Jupiter	♌	1
♄	Saturn	♑	6
♅	Uranus	♌	12
♆	Neptune	♈	9
♇	Pluto	♉	10
⚷	Chiron	♈	9
⚶	Vesta	♍	2
⚴	Pallas	♐	4
✴	Juno	♏	3
⚳	Ceres	♐	5
⚚	Hygeia	♐	4
☊	North Node	♊	10
☋	South Node	♐	4
⊗	Pt Fortune	♈	8

ASPECTS

☊	☍	☋	0°00' S		☊	✶	⊗	0°29' A
☿	△	♄	0°00' S		☋	△	⊗	0°29' A
♀	⚼	♄	0°00' S		♀	✶	✴	0°34' A
☽	⚻	♂	0°08' S		☿	∠	✴	0°35' S
♂	⚼	⚴	0°10' A		☽	☌	⚳	0°48' A
♃	⚼	⚳	0°15' S		☉	⚼	⊗	0°49' S

Supportive aspects:

    Conjunction—Alliance

    Trine—Empowering support

    Sextile—Symbiosis

    Quintile—Creative stimulation

Challenging aspects:

    Teaching moments that build our soul's muscles

    Opposition—Confrontation

    Square—Collision

    Semi-square—Irritation

    Quincunx—Challenging stretch

Chart patterns:

    Concentration within the four hemispheres, where your energy concentrates

    Stellium—Busy house with three or more planets teaming up

Bowl—All the planets in one hemisphere
Cup/bucket—All the planets in one hemisphere
except for one
Bundle—All the planets close together
Locomotion—Planets evenly spaced, heading in
a direction
Splay/splash—Planets every which way
Seesaw—Two groups of planets that balance each other

CHALLENGING ASPECTS: THE TEACHERS

"May you integrate all your squares" is an astrological blessing.

The hard or challenging aspects of an opposition (180 degrees apart) or a square (90 degrees apart) can act like a martial-arts teacher, one who challenges you to step up, get stronger, work through karma, and develop your talents. They can also act as diversity training for your inner company, because when disparate elements with different backgrounds and agendas, like the planets in a square or opposition, learn to work together, there is not much they cannot do. Together they can create a more cohesive and multitalented whole and build up resilience to handle the world.

Using another useful metaphor, challenging aspects act like a combustion engine; the very tension of them can drive us forward. And like a combustion engine, if you time it right, these explosions give you the power to get where you need to go. If it's not well coordinated, those miniature explosions can blow up the whole engine.

MAJOR CHALLENGING ASPECTS

- Square (90 degrees, one fourth of the way around the circle)
- Oppositions (180 degrees, one half of the way around the circle)

MINOR CHALLENGING ASPECTS

- Semi-square (45 degrees, one eighth of the way around the circle), two- to three-degree orb
- Semi-sextiles (30 degrees, one twelfth of the way around the circle), two- to three-degree orb
- Quincunx (150 degrees), three- to five-degree orb

Opposition: Confrontation

An opposition is formed by two planets on either side of the circles. They focus upon one another intensely, like sparring partners at a wrestling match. The Sun and Moon oppose each other at every full Moon, and it highlights that intense relationship and differences between our conscious mind, the Sun, and our unconscious and emotional realm, the Moon. These two planets are in the same polarity, so they have a language in common. But somehow, you were probably trained to believe that you had to choose between one energy or the other, between mother or father, between mind and feelings, and it will be up to you to create your own map to integrate the energy of these two planets. Help these two elements compete less and work better together.

Square: Competition

A square is formed by two planets at right angles to each other. Usually in the same modality as each other, either cardinal, fixed, or mutable, these two planets can compete like siblings. Imagine that you are standing at a crossroads, holding the reins to two horses, each one pulling in a different direction, competing for your attention and potentially leaving you stuck at the crossroads. If you can just get the horses going in the same direction, rather than competing over you, think of the momentum you could build. These two planets are usually in the same modality, cardinal fixed or mutable, but do not share polarity or element. They don't speak the same language.

The trick is to get the parts of your personality represented by these squared planets to respect one another rather than compete, to support the differences between their needs rather than deny them or give up.

For example, let's say your Mercury, which symbolizes your thinking and communication abilities, squares Saturn, the rigorous, organized, sometimes-restricted planet that likes rules and hard work. Your rapid-moving mind can feel at odds with your need for security, stability, proof, and discipline. You could have a fear of being trapped, but your mind may have trouble letting go. Mercury squares Saturn can help you hold on tenaciously to your thoughts, which can be difficult in dinner-party banter or when you are obsessing on a problem at 2 A.M., but when you get that Mercury and Saturn to work together, you can develop a mind that perseveres. Together they could help you write a book, get an advanced degree, or build a company.

Minor Challenging Aspects: Irritations

The semi-square, which is 45 degrees apart; a semi-sextile, which is one sign apart; and the quincunx, which is five signs apart, are all minor tense aspects that irritate and cause inconvenience. They occur between two points with nothing in common—not polarity, not modality, not element. These are your inner diversity training aspects. You may see less obvious tension between the sides, but it will take some conscious effort to help these elements work together within you. In doing so, they build up strength and broaden your perspective.

To dive deeper into your own chart, write down the key teachers in your chart, your challenging aspects. Start with the major aspects, your oppositions and squares, and riff on what difficulties they represent. Describe what you have learned from these teachers, both from challenges they've offered and what you have learned about reconciling their different needs and agenda.

There are other, more subtle—but still challenging—aspects, but get to know these first.

SUPPORTIVE ASPECTS

Soft or supporting aspects create connections, alliances, and friendships. You can think of these like combinations of best buddies who stand behind you, and work with you, but they might not tell you some tough truths. These planets symbiotically work together, and their abilities mesh easily with one another.

Lean in to your supportive aspects, but don't take them for granted. Like a friend who is there for you but may not challenge you when you need it, they can make life easier for you as they impart flow, ease, and talent. Easy aspects can also bring laziness. They don't necessarily build strength—that's for you to do.

Think of them like an inheritance, because they are a cosmic inheritance from the stars and from your other lives. What do you want to do with your inheritance? There is no wrong answer. Only you know what's best for your soul. For example, say, three people inherit a chunk of money. One person decides that's good enough, and they'll just sit by the pool and enjoy that ease for the rest of their life. Some people do just need a life to rest. Another takes the inheritance for granted, thinks this lifestyle is normal and everybody with less is deficient, looks down on those without that chunk of money, even though they did nothing to build it, and squanders it away. But the third person might take that inheritance as a cosmic arts grant and use that to dive into their art form or invest in work that grows more resources for themselves and others. Consider carefully what you want to do with your supportive aspects.

The major supportive aspects are the conjunction, where two planets run together, trines with each planet one third of the way around the zodiac from the other and the sextile.

MAJOR SUPPORTIVE ASPECTS

- Conjunction—0 degrees
- Trine (120 degrees, one third of the way around the circle), 8- to 10-degree orb
- Sextile (60 degrees, one sixth of the way around the circle)

MINOR SUPPORTIVE ASPECTS

- Quintile (72 degrees, one fifth of the way around the circle), two- to three-degree orb

Conjunction: Alliance

In a conjunction two planets hold hands and dance together; their actions yoke together and blend their meaning and purpose. The Sun and Moon conjunct on a New Moon and begin a new lunar cycle. Every conjunction begins a new evolutionary and experiential cycle. When two planets yoke together in a conjunction, they become greater than the sum of their parts and are a real power source in the chart.

Though a conjunction can be a little tricky if it involves the Sun because the Sun is so huge, the planet appears to disappear into it, or becomes combust as it approaches or leaves the Sun. A combust planet flavors the nature of the Sun's light but loses its identity and independent action. If it is in the heart of the Sun, within a degree of the Sun, it is called Cazimi, in which case that planet glows with extra strength and power, as if the sunlight pours through that planet.

Trines and Sextiles: Symbiosis

Trines are formed by planets around the same degree, one third of the way around the zodiac, so they form two corners of an equilateral triangle. Trines are strongest when they are in the same element—fire, Earth, air, or water—where they'll be in different modalities but will speak the same language.

Sextiles are formed by planets in one sixth of the way around the zodiac in nearby signs of the same polarity, either yin (water and Earth) or yang (fire and air), and so work easily together. Planets that sextile one another can be like Butch Cassidy and the Sundance Kid, or Thelma and Louise: in a buddy relationship where the supportive differences add to the gift. These planets have each other's back and enjoy palling around.

As an example, if your Mercury, which rules the mind and communications ability, trines Uranus, a planet of ingenuity and invention, you tend to think fast, even have the spark of brilliance, and work well with inventive technology but may have trouble with patience or mental discipline. If your Mercury sextiles Venus, your mind and your sense of aesthetics or compassion work together comfortably, which can give you a lovely voice and poetic expression, though maybe you'd prefer not to talk about difficult things.

The quintile is a minor and supportive aspect one fifth of the way around the circle and one corner of a pentacle. Pentacles and the number five are related to Venus. This aspect stimulates a creative gift.

Write down the key "buddies" in your chart, your encouraging aspects. Start with the Sun and Moon, and then in order of proximity to the Sun: Mercury, Venus, Mars, Jupiter, Saturn, Uranus, Neptune, and Pluto. List the conjunctions first, then trines and sextile, then quintile. These are your resources, the points in your chart of easy flow and special gifts. Contemplate what gifts they bring you.

An applying aspect, one where that light grows stronger every hour until it is exact, occurs where the faster-moving planet approaches the slower-moving planet. Applying aspects have a larger orb than a separating aspect. An applying aspect in your natal chart can describe a story that will unfold in your early life.

A separating aspect has already hit its peak, and although we can still see and feel that beam of connection, it fades every hour. Separating aspect refers to a talent, attitude, or concern that you arrived with in this life, as if the story or development happened in another lifetime. You can often find a story that echoes this pattern, which happened in your family before you were born.

My theory is that separating aspects point to soul work that started in another lifetime and continues in this one, but you don't need to know the story to do the work. For example, if you died in the middle of a battlefield, you might be born in the middle of a family feud; the details are different, but the soul work is similar. The planets ask you to reconcile, heal, and learn from conflict. Never take this as an excuse to think someone deserved the pain they are going through, as we do not know the story. When you see a separating difficult aspect, drop assumptions and honor that challenge with respect and support.

We usually give the Sun and Moon 11 degrees approaching, and 8 degrees leaving. Jupiter is close, because it is so big, 10 to 8 degrees, and the rest of the planets around 8 to 6 degrees, though every astrologer may have a different experience with them.

Super Aspects: A Meeting of the Planets

When more than two planets are involved, the pattern takes on more power and significance.

Stellium: A super conjunction. A stellium occurs when three or more planets gather close together, either conjunct in the same sign or concentrated in the same house. Such focus and concentration in your chart is a well you can draw from. What you draw from that well depends on the sign, the house, and the planets involved, but consider it a powerful reserve. But it can be hard to understand that concentration, that gift, because it's just you, like how a fish swimming in water can't see the water. It may be helpful to develop the skills associated with the sign involved (or the sign opposite it). For example, if you have four planets in the twelfth house, it will help you to develop your sixth house pragmatic healthy daily habits, skills for dealing with the world to help you unpack and use the potentially strong intuitive and insightful gift of the twelfth house.

Grand trine: A super trine that is three planets in the same element, each one third of the way around the circle, together forming a triangle. Grand trines are stable and powerful energy builders. As this creates a place of ease, comfort and power within a chart, the person will tend to lean on their grand trine and do what is easiest for them along that line. The nature of that stability will depend on whether this is a fire, Earth, air, or water grand trine. Think back to your elements. If you have a grand trine, lean in to this gift of yours. Those three planets work together and speak the same language. But you may need to consciously develop the rest of the chart to round yourself out; it can be easier to avoid the harder soul work when you have a place where things seem to flow. Rather than avoid them, use that flow to tackle your challenges.

Grand square: Four planets are at right angles to one another and form the four corners of a grand square. This is most powerful if they are all in the same modality—cardinal, fixed, or mutable—and represent a super concentration of that mode. If you have a grand, the parts of your personality they represent can feel at all odds, fighting or frustrating one another in the process. You will not have a map from your family of origin for how to get these disparate elements to work together; that's something for you to find on your own. You can no more choose which corner to live out than you can choose which leg to stand upon. You must find a map in your mind for how these parts can support one another and take turns. Timeshare between these skills and interests. If you can get all those parts of you to agree on a common goal, grand squares are often found in the most successful ambitious charts.

T-square: Two planets that oppose one another and both square a third corner—three corners of a square—can build up the same kind of energy as a grand square. But all that energy can form a parabolic mirror, concentrate the energy, and focus on the missing corner as if it's a ghost planet. Look to the house where the fourth planet would be to complete a square and notice that this makes a good focus to get the other three planets to work together.

Grand sextile: Six planets, each 60 degrees apart, form grand trines—a powerful, positive chart that seems to have good flow. However, it is often found in the charts of someone who has abig challenge either elsewhere in the chart or in their lives. The trick will be to use the flow to handle the challenge, not hide from it. If you have five planets sextile one another, and you are missing one corner of the grand sextile, like a T-square, that missing point can take the focus and act as a catalyst, but you may have to consciously engage it.

Yod: Sometimes called the finger of God, the yod is formed by two planets who sextile each other, and both quincunx or form an irritating 150-degree aspect to a third planet across the chart. Two points of ease, the sextiles, provide a strength that focuses to solve a problem, the irritant on the other side. This can be a powerful aspect of fate and purpose, like a beckoning finger that says, "Here. Do the work here. Apply your talents here."

Astrological Signs			Aspects	
♈ Aries	♉ Taurus	♊ Gemini	♂	Conjunction
♋ Cancer	♌ Leo	♍ Virgo	☍	Opposition
♎ Libra	♏ Scorpio	♐ Sagittarius	△	Trine
♑ Capricorn	♒ Aquarius	♓ Pisces	□	Square

Planets						Semi-sextile
☉	Sun	☽	Moon	☿	Mercury	⚹ Sextile
♀	Venus	♂	Mars	♃	Jupiter	⊼ Inconjunct
♄	Saturn	♅	Uranus	♆	Neptune	∠ Semi-square
♇	Pluto	☊	North Node	☋	South Node	⊡ Sesqui-quadrate
⚷	Chiron	⚴	Pallas	⚵	Juno	✳ Septile
⚳	Ceres	⚶	Vesta	⊕	Earth	⋈ Novile

Importance	First		Second	Third				Fourth	
Aspect	Conjunc-tion	Opposi-tion	Square	Trine	Sextile	Semi-sextile	Quincunx	Quintile
Glyph	♂	☍	□	△	✳	ⅴ	⊼	Q
Angle	0°	180°	90°	120°	60°	30°	150°	72°
Fraction	0/2	1/2	1/4	1/3	1/6	1/12	5/12	1/5
Regular Polygon	Monogon	Digon	Square	Triangle	Hexagon	Dodecagon	Dodecagram	Pentagon

Let's weave these aspects into that star quilt of your chart. Each planet and aspect offers another layer, another piece of that quilt. Most charts are full of interesting contradictions, and that's what makes you unique. If one aspect gives you articulation, and another makes you self-conscious, know that the situation will depend on which aspect is being triggered at the moment by transits and the circumstances herein and how the other aspects support or challenge that skill.

ASPECTS FROM THE PLANETS

Mercury

Supportive aspects between the Moon and Mercury at your birth help your mind and heart work together. They bring mental agility, give you a special charismatic touch, and help you find the right words to reach the public. You can be clever, witty, often charming and creative, and can excel at any job where you need to think fast and respond on the spot. But if you don't want to be just glib, you have to choose depth. Even though you learn quickly, you need to look below the surface and search for meaning if you actually want wisdom.

Challenging aspects between the Moon and Mercury at your birth add mental agility and brilliance but can make your learning process a little peculiar; you have to find the learning style that works for you. You can get anxious or worried if you focus on what could go wrong without considering what could go right. Sometimes your mind doesn't know how to shut off and keeps the brain's hamster wheel going all night unless you find ways to relax the mind. You can communicate eloquently, but sometimes it can feel so important to be heard that you become impatient with the process of dialogue. This improves with age.

Help for your Mercury: If you feel the tension between the Moon and Mercury and feel nervous or torn between an emotional and logical response, let your heart and mind have a good talk with one another. Pretend they sit on either side of the room and speak from your mind to the heart, then from the heart to the mind, and mediate dialogue between them. On a more pragmatic level, games of mental focus or meditation can help you focus, as does any exercise to lower your stress level and realign your nervous system. Acupuncture, yoga, and all efforts at stress relief will help you tap into this scintillating potential.

Venus

Supportive aspects between the Moon and Venus at your birth infuse you with grace and charm and can soften many otherwise hard aspects of the chart. Beauty is not optional for you. Although Venus has generally expensive tastes, and you probably can walk into a store and choose the most expensive item there, it really is more about the aesthetics than the cost; you can create beauty wherever you go. Because people like you, they tend to give you things, so this aspect adds luck. Your hopes, fears, and excitement about relationships can take up a large part of your emotional landscape. You network easily and people tend to remember you. You're good at hooking up others for work or love because you understand the nature of connections. You have a seductive quality, so use your powers for good.

Challenging aspects between the Moon and Venus at your birth can give you charm with attitude. People may be drawn to you, but you may have little respect for social niceties and grow twitchy under attempts at social pleasantries. You may be the brooding artist in the corner who everybody wants to talk to or collect too many beautiful things to make you comfortable. Own up to the fact that you're more social than you admit but are not really secure in your lovability. You'd prefer others to make the first overture and so make connection safe for you. Really, you feel for others and don't want to hurt anyone, but sometimes your self-protection does just that. The more you own your Venus, your warmth and kindness, the more comfortable you become in social situations and the more beautiful you may feel.

Help for your Venus: If you feel the tension between the Moon and Venus, you may be tempted to do some retail therapy. Consider creating beauty rather than buying it, because if you keep importing it, not only will you be broke, but you may never quite feed the hunger. Or when your heart feels like it's on hot coals, express affection and compassion: hug a dog, be kind to a neighbor, connect with a lonely soul so your own heart can calm down.

Mars

Supportive aspects between the Moon and Mars at your birth add power to your mood and assertiveness to your demeanor. You probably had some muscle-building experiences as a kid and had to roll with conflict or manage strong personalities that taught you to stand up for yourself. You are familiar and comfortable with strong women. Often you see what needs to be done and have the energy to get the ball rolling. Engage your ability to be an advocate for the weak, one who speaks up and says what needs to be said. Just watch a tendency to run roughshod over less-assertive types.

Challenging aspects between the Moon and Mars at your birth builds a strong inner combustion engine and drives you to keep moving and get things done. You may have started out brilliant and had a powerful adolescence but may have taken time to recalibrate and redirect as an adult. Because you adapted to willful personalities as a kid, sometimes you order other people around; at a job where firm leadership is required, this is wonderful, but it may need to be dialed back in a relationship. Your inner adolescent is enthusiastic but always ready to come out and get pugnacious. You probably came by your defensiveness with good cause and developed a protective chip on your shoulder but now have to ask yourself if it will still serve you.

Help for your Mars: If you feel the tension between the Moon and Mars and find yourself angry, irritable, or accident prone, first work out—find a good outlet for your physical energy so it doesn't swirl into tension or temper. Then find a way to develop your role as guardian, the positive refrain for militancy. It's easy to do this in the military or as a police officer, but you can also use this guardian capacity to protect family, business, or health, or be a champion for a worthy cause. Just make sure those people want guarding.

Jupiter

Supportive aspects from Jupiter at your birth imbue a philosophical perspective and a general philanthropic desire to see the good in people, to believe if we just keep the conversation going, we can get to the bottom of things. Publicity and respect come easily to you. You may not always respect boundaries and may be surprised when other people don't share your magnanimous views. Your approach is so natural to you, you have trouble understanding people who take moral shortcuts or get bitter instead of active. But you can help other people see the good in them themselves and help us all find the silver lining.

Challenging aspects from Jupiter at your birth are still pretty wonderful. You keep the charm, the luck, the natural sense of bounty and an ability to return to optimism, which can soften harder aspects in your chart, but you need to watch a tendency to overdo or be over-trusting. Whatever planet or house Jupiter challenges can expand and lose proportion, inflame, overflow, or overdo unless you have a clear healthy outlet for this bounty.

Help for your Jupiter: It can be easy to get stuck in our Jupiter aspects and forget to develop the more difficult or muscular parts of our chart. If you feel like you are overindulging or giving too much and no one else is giving back, investigate how to give yourself the gift of balance. If you find there is too much of an outside influence, whether that's a parent, work, or whatever is exacerbated by Jupiter, learn to set healthy limits on that outside influence. Find a joyful and productive outlet for your own abundance, whatever you have too much of—too much energy, too much love, too many business skills—and balance the rest of your life to hold that aperture open in a good way.

Saturn

Supportive aspects from Saturn at your birth can bring you maturity at an early age. For some reason you had to take the world seriously and develop competence early. People may have thought you were older than you were as a child; learning how to play could be your challenge. You may be wary of agreeing to do something because you take your responsibilities seriously. If you let yourself build skill over time, you can become highly skilled and build mastery. You do your homework, apprentice well, and learn by doing.

Challenging aspects from Saturn can be a seriously motivating aspect. Because you see the long road ahead and all the bumps in it, it can be hard for you to let yourself be a beginner. Saturn loans seriousness and competence over time, but can also bring depression or discouragement. You can be competent, serious, but driven by a haunting concern that what you do is not enough and who you are will never be enough. If you decide to be miserable, you do that with equal success. It's up to you. But consider ignoring other people's expectations and listening to your inner calling. Take that one step at a time and accomplish what matters to you.

Help for your Saturn: If you feel uncomfortable because your world feels out of control, or you feel too driven to relax, make self-care your goal. Choose to be ambitious about your health, calmness, and contentment, and make plans within your control. You can then build from that place of organization and stability.

Uranus

Supportive aspects from Uranus add brilliance, humor, nervous energy, eccentricity, and the ability to think outside the box. As a matter of fact, it may be hard for you to think inside the box about the nature of the other aspected planets. You think for yourself. You may be more at home with technology than some and have a naturally cross-referencing mind. Slowing your nervous system down to connect with others may be a bit of a challenge. Have patience for people who work at a different rhythm.

Challenging aspects from Uranus add brilliance and impulsiveness, but you need to add control. Naturally inventive, you may have trouble learning the ordinary steps or following conventional etiquette. Here you can jump to conclusions and sound arrogant, whether or not you know what you're talking about. Here you are naturally inventive but can be eternally restless.

Help for your Uranus: If you feel nervous or easily discontent, work with your nervous system. Use meditation, tai chi, Reiki, any of the healing arts that help direct nervous energy so it works for you and not against you. When you're in a situation that you can't change, think about what you can change, find allies who see that change is necessary, and put your energy there. Give yourself one place in your life where you can invent at your own pace without consensus from others.

Neptune

Supportive aspects from Neptune add a dreamy quality to your personality, a creative mystique. You may appreciate a strong intuitive connection with your beloveds. Here your sensitivities become your gift. Neptune can add inspiration to discipline, can give you a dream worth working toward. It can also imbue you with a certain ephemeral magic and a tendency to work outside of normal schedules and linear time. This is a place where you need inspiration. Neptune loans you a gift to work with water, liquid, and oils, with the sea and stream, with myth and story.

Challenging aspects from Neptune can make reality ephemeral. Here you may feel like an intuitive sponge and need to learn where your feelings begin and theirs end. Here you can pick up so much from your environment, you could feel overwhelmed. Harsh sounds and ugly sights grate on your nerves. You need time out, but watch that escapist streak. Learn to tell the difference between your prodigious imagination and your active intuition; they can all jumble up within. Feed your need for magic with healthy fantasy or good book. Put your imagination to good use.

Help for your Neptune: If you feel overwhelmed or lost, it helps to take a two-pronged approach. First honor your Neptune and create an altar or prayer space and call for spiritual help; call on your guides and guardians and the best of your ancestors for support. Or dive into your creative work and let your imagination roam. Be careful with drugs or alcohol, as you may be unusually susceptible to their swamp, and while they provide a temporary break, they will make your reality harder to return to. For the second prong, imagine a life wonderful enough to stay present within, dream up the next step, and then walk forward.

Pluto

Supportive aspects to Pluto add reserve, depth, breadth, and, when you come to terms with Pluto, the strength to handle real problems. You may have earned this in your childhood through being there for yourself through lonely times when parents or caretakers were distracted or difficult. If there's a problem, you probably want to look at it squarely in the face, which gives you a special talent for work where depth and presence are required. You may be bored by ordinary life and friendly people on a good day and small talk can leave you cold, but bring up the challenge and you're right there.

Challenging aspects to Pluto can give you the same depth and breadth, but you may either get stuck in the depths or be the one to create the problem. If you created it, then you are not out of control. You may have a slightly morbid streak and be curious about dire events, but this is part of your training to cope. An obsessive-compulsive streak can kick in under stress. You can be volcanic or implode when angry and are particularly triggered by all the Pluto issues: abuse of vulnerability, oppression, and misuse of power. If friends tell you to lighten up, they don't get your gift. Enjoy your solitude but do not isolate. Pluto can occasionally bring real mental health issues from tangible trauma. If so, seek the help you need to heal.

Help for your Pluto: Explore the depths, look at the worst-case scenarios, and know you could deal with it and therefore can look for the best-case scenarios. Therapy can be fascinating as a way of exploring the corners of the psyche and developing new understanding. Make a radical act of compassion; if your heart hurts, go hug every dog at the pound and listen to their stories. Tap into a real need and find a way to be helpful. Paradoxically, you could calm down when working on the front lines or tackling real problems.

PLANETARY CONTAINMENT—
ASTROLOGICAL NEIGHBORS

Once you're born, the pattern of your planets is set in place. Every month the Moon will go around the zodiac, go around your chart, and illuminate these planets in the same order. Every year the Sun, Mercury, and Venus do the same. Though you are working with a circle without a beginning or an end, your chart does have an intrinsic pattern. We learned a lot about our experience with the planet by looking at the planet before it in the zodiac and the planet afterward.

This pattern of astrological neighbors is most noticeable if these planets are right next door—for example, if you have a Sun-Venus-Mars conjunction, these three planets clearly work together. It is less noticeable if these neighbors are two signs part. But they are still set off in this rhythm every time a planet goes by.

To learn more about the influences on any planet, after you've noticed the major aspects coming to and from that planet, check out its neighborhood. Notice the planet right before it on the zodiac and the one right afterward, no matter how far away. The first planet before passes them the light, and the other takes it, as if they are always running a relay race or passing a ball. Look to the planet beforehand as the trigger, doorway, or segue into this planet's action. Then look at the planet afterward for where that planet shares its light and how it takes action in response.

Let's go back and look at the chart for Sri Aurobindo for an example. If we want to know more about his Mars—his temper and his physicality—we notice that Mars is contained by Pluto on one side, and Uranus on the other. So his experience of powerful authority figures, represented by Pluto in the tenth, affects his temper, his boundaries, and his physicality, and leads him to create change, with Uranus on the other side. Over his lifetime he went to from working hard, first for the English government of India, then for Indian rebellion and independence. Later on, he took his experience in dealing with Pluto power struggles and turned it toward Plutonian empowerment of himself and others as he stepped into his own authority as a writer and teacher. He taught integral yoga—a high note of Mars—with the goal to help people change their health and awareness, represented by Mars and Uranus together in the twelfth house.

Now look at his Sun, his core personality, contained by Jupiter and Venus. Every month the Moon would hit his Jupiter first—asking him to expand his heart and perception, broaden his horizons, and bring that expanded perspective to his Sun. His core personality then expresses that with creativity, compassion, and charisma as it passes the light over to Venus.

In your chart, take a look at the order of your planets. Start with a few basics like your Sun and Moon. Look at the planets before and after them in the zodiac. Ruminate on this and tell a story about how the planet before handles your Sun, your core essence, stories, energy, experience, and light, and how your Sun, your personality, may pass that on or express it through the next planet afterward. What are the disadvantages and advantages of this pattern?

CHART PATTERNS

Step back now and look at the overall pattern of the chart. What is your first impression? Do you see planets scattered evenly around the chart? Are they focused together in one place? Do they have a concentration on one side with one or two planets balancing it on the other? Are they all grouped together in one quadrant? Are they concentrated, balanced, scattered? Personalities echo those patterns. Your emotional impression of these patterns is probably astrologically accurate. There is no good pattern or bad pattern, but the chart makeup helps us see the concentration and the emphasis, the weight of the planets in the psyche. It is always easier to work with one's basic nature and energy profile and then expand ourselves from there. Overall patterns in the chart help us understand where our inspiration comes from and what we might need to round ourselves out.

As this is a circle, quadrant one is not less evolved than quadrant four. Our life consciousness and experience spin through all these quadrants as the transits illuminate the far corners of our chart. Our job is always to complete the mandala and round out our understanding.

A concentration in anyone part of the chart brings a focused gift, but to use that gift clearly you may need to consciously develop the house and sign opposite the concentration to unpack it and engage those talents. You may be drawn to people whose charts hold planets that fill in your empty areas, or you might draw in experiences that act out and enrich those quiet corners of our chart. Souls long for wholeness.

First let's look at the hemispheres and the quadrants. You can think of them like neighborhoods in a town, divided by a river, which is the horizon.

Hemispheres

With the Eastern hemisphere, on the side of the ascendant, the energy starts from within. Some thought, feeling, or impulse arises from the soul's personal perspective, and they bring it out to the world. If the bulk or emphasis is in the Western hemisphere, anchored by the descendant, events happen as the person engages the world that trigger an internal response. Either way you can get the work done, but it can be helpful to understand the evolutionary triggers.

The hemisphere above the horizon of the Earth, where the Sun would be during the day, is in the realm of consciousness and worldly interaction, and adds extraversion and curiosity. Emphasis in the hemisphere below the horizon adds a layer of introversion and introspection. The soul grows through the realm of personal investigation, family, and personal relationships.

Quadrants

The quadrants are formed by the interaction between these two hemispheres and follow logically.

Quadrant 1, where the Sun would be from midnight to sunrise and runs between the ascendant and the IC, emphasizes self-discovery. It establishes how you create that identity through how you present yourself, how you relate to your body, and how you learn. Growth starts with personal exploration, then this personality triggers events in the world around them. From this awareness of themselves, their resources, and their neighborhood, they can engage the world. A heavy emphasis in this quadrant says you are on a journey of self-discovery and that your identity arises from within. You are the gift you offer to the world and you have the ability to articulate what you have to offer.

Quadrant 2, where the Sun would be from sunset to midnight, runs between the IC and the descendant and emphasizes personal relationships through family, love affairs, and co-workers as the place where growth begins. With an emphasis in this quadrant, a person could learn so much through their relationship to family, children, romance, or creative process that they are inspired to become a good therapist or teacher. Their story starts with the personal, then extends out to the world.

Quadrant 3, where the Sun would be from noon to sunset, from the descendant to the midheaven, is probably the most public area, often well developed in comfortably sociable business people. Here ideas and evolution begin in that interaction with the bigger world, and here they have real skill. Those worldly relationships can spark introspection and a journey inward.

Quadrant 4, where the Sun dwells from sunrise to noon, which runs between your midheaven and your ascendant, speaks of both our most public and private selves and holds how you metabolize your experiences in maturity.

Here you integrate your interactions and bring them back to your own path. It is the fruit on your tree, what you have created and offer back to the world in your professions, community involvement, your circle and your sangha, from this life and previous ones. It is what you do behind the scenes and deep within your spiritual practice. A loaded fourth quadrant suggests you can thoughtfully balance your responsibilities and your inward search.

Next we will talk about how the planets are distributed around your chart and what those patterns might tell you about how your psyche is organized.

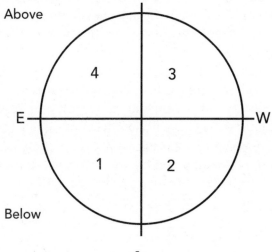

PLANETARY PATTERNS

Although astrologers have been looking at these patterns for millennia, the astrologer Marc Edmund Jones, active in the mid-1900s, developed the names for specific patterns and researched what these patterns meant. But your intuitive, overall impression will probably tell you the same thing.

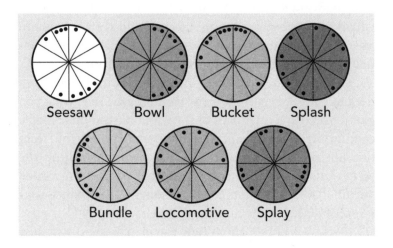

Seesaw   Bowl   Bucket   Splash

Bundle   Locomotive   Splay

Splash or scatter pattern occurs where the planets are splashed all over the circle with no concentration in any one house or sign. This pattern brings an extra level of versatility and diversity. Some part of this person can talk to anyone. This chart can feel like the jack-of-all-trades, with a little bit of skill in a lot of places and the gift of being able to see how they all fit together. If your chart has this scatter pattern, versatility and adaptability could be your superpowers, though you may have trouble deciding on one course of action. Because it furthers to round out the personality, see if you can both appreciate this versatility and develop your ability to concentrate. Focus on a handful of things, maybe three or four projects, rather than 20. Develop a day where you spend a few hours on one skill or interest, a few hours on another, rather than trying to choose only one. If you try to do just one thing, the other parts of your personality will complain and undermine it. Your soul chose this versatility for reason, so embrace and focus this versatility and give all parts of you room to express.

The **splay or tripod pattern** has three concentrations. These concentrations can act like a cyclotron and build great energy to move forward if those three corners can find a way to relate to each other. If, for example, your mind disrespects your love life, which disrespects your craft, as represented by your chart, you may run around among the three, each interest undermining the other, rather than building a healthy rapport. Do not try to choose between these three concentrations, but make them relevant to one another, respect each concentration, and make sure there is time in your life for all three corners. A tripod can be a very stable and dynamic structure.

The **train track or locomotive pattern** has planets fairly evenly spaced but all heading in one direction, with one third of the chart empty. The first planet after the empty space, the one that would rise after the empty space, is considered the locomotion of the train, the planet that drives the rest of the chart. It acts as a co-ruler of the chart, no matter what sign is on the ascendant. This chart can feel as driven or determined as a long-distance train.

The **bowl** contains all the planets in 180 degrees, one hemisphere, and can provoke two reactions. This chart will tend to be self-contained, like a bowl, and hold all of its interests and focus calmly in that bowl and choose to stay there. But that bowl can also act like a parabolic mirror and collect light and energy to focus on the empty corner. Look to the midpoint opposite the bowl.

The bundle is like the bowl but even more concentrated. All the planets are within 120 degrees, or in one third of the chart. This chart has even more focus and less interest in diversifying or filling out the opposite sides. It can feel in this chart like the person is bringing forth a body of work from another lifetime. That person is here to complete the work, repair those relationships, and they don't really appreciate distractions.

The cup/bucket holds all the planets in one hemisphere but one singleton planet opposite, which acts like the handle to that cup or bucket. That planet can be like a lightning rod and bring in experiences that charge and catalyze the rest of the chart and can also become the nozzle by which the chart expresses itself into the world. Since there is such a strong sense of calling around that point, although their life may look like a winding path, it will keep recentering on an expression of that singleton planet.

The seesaw pattern is formed by two bundles or concentrations of planets on either side of the chart, which balance each other out. This pattern can act like a giant opposition in the chart, where the person feels like they need to be one or the other, A or B, which creates tension or can leave them feeling stuck at the crossroads. They do not have a map from the family of origin on how to balance and live out both sides of the same time, but that is where their gift unfolds. Find a third position, a purpose and way of life that both sides can engage in, and this can be a powerful chart.

Let's look at an example of these patterns. Go back to Sri Aurobindo's chart on page 156 and notice he has a splayed pattern, a tripod with three focuses of concentration. His chart is fairly balanced between east and west, with one of the luminaries, Sun and Moon, in either hemisphere. He has more planets below the horizon than above, but not a huge preponderance. It does suggest that his experience is personal. He develops an awareness within and with the people that he knows and loves, and then takes it out to change the world.

Look at your chart in an abstract way; just notice the pattern and shape created by the planets and asteroids in your chart. Write down your impression of the movement, the gifts, and the challenges of the patterns the planets create. Then, after this first impression, think about which category your chart might fit in. Note the hemisphere and quadrant emphasized and ponder how this fits your experience of your life. If you have the charts of people you know well, compare these patterns and note the differences.

CHANGING STATES: TRANSITS AND PROGRESSIONS

Your natal chart can be seen as your musical instrument, your piano, that resonating pattern formed when you breathed into this life.

But the starry heavens do not hold still. The planets are always moving through time and space, living out their cycles, spinning around us. When those planets form geometric relationships to one another, they create the daily or mundane transits, the astrological weather conditions of our time, changing slowly through each minute of the day.

And like any weather conditions, we react differently depending upon our needs. The farmer with a parched field will be glad to see a rainstorm approach, but a lover planning a picnic or a child with a playdate could be deeply disappointed. If you are feeling bored and longing for a change, but no shift in your life is in sight, an approaching Uranus transit may be just the exciting train that can take you to a new chapter in your life. If you really like where you are and don't want anything to shift, that Uranus transit can be daunting and will need careful management so that you can direct the control in a good way. And even then, Uranus can deal us a wildcard that only makes sense in retrospect.

Astrologers use many systems to track the changes on your chart, and each system could take several books to explain in detail and years of observation to implement. I'll touch on a few here and then go into more in-depth for transits and progressions.

Transits track where the planets are today in relationship to your natal chart. Each passing planet lights up your chart with its own music and plays their own tunes on that original piano of your natal chart.

Progressions follow the map etched by the transits of your first few months of life, a pattern that stretches out the overall landscape of your life. You live this pattern out, with a lot of choice about how, for the rest of your life. Secondary progressions, the system I use most, unroll this map at the rate of roughly one day of your early life to one year of your life's overall flow. Tertiary progressions unroll that map at the rate of one day of your early life to one month of your life's overall flow. All these patterns echo together in an empowering, symbolic way. You get to choose how you live out those symbols.

The time lord or chronocrator systems of traditional astrology use several methods to figure out the rhythm and timing of your life, periods of time where the planets trade off leadership of your life like a relay race, which are regular cycles set in motion at the time of your birth. The cycles progress at the same rate for everyone, but are changed by the nature of your relationship to that planet at the beginning. If you had a comfortable Saturn in your natal chart, your Saturn transits can be empowering and scientific, and ultimately successful for your work. If your relationship to Saturn in your natal chart was less beneficent, then that cycle can bring more heavy lifting. In my experience, the time lord systems set a background, and the play on the stage can be seen through transits and progressions. Who the time lord of a particular time in your life is depends on which system you are using at the moment; an Internet search will provide several calculators.

Solar arc progressions: The Sun moves forward about one degree a day. In solar arc progressions, all the planets are asked to follow the Sun, and so move forward one degree for every year of a person's life. If, for example, your Mars is at 0 degrees of Leo, and your Sun is at 23 degrees of Leo, then when you are 23 years old, your solar arc Mars would conjunct your natal Sun, and you might need to do something extra with your energy that year, take on a healthy challenge, and use the positive edge of Mars.

Any of these systems need to be layered onto a real understanding of your natal chart, so always start there first. In my experience, the transits are the easiest to learn, track, and experience and teach you more about your natal chart as you follow along.

TRANSITS: CHANGING CLIMATE

Sometimes you can just listen to a person talk about their life and predict what planet is talking to their chart, and what transits they are experiencing. If everything is foggy and boundaries are difficult to achieve, and they just lost their car keys this morning, look for a Neptune transit. If they are experiencing a slow but deep existential angst, wondering what the purpose of life is, and have had to recently let go of important people or things, look for a Pluto transit. Those aspects are not inevitable from those planets but are often a surefire sign they are involved.

Finding your transits used to be somewhat complicated: you had to know your chart and where the planets are today, using a planetary ephemeris or astrological calendar, and then apply them to your natal chart. But nowadays you can just do an Internet search for transits, and good astrological sites offer a printout with transit timing and basic information. Most astrological apps for your phone can also give you an image of your basic chart with the transits around the outside.

Decades ago, we had a more mechanical way of learning the transits. If you are interested in really getting to know astrology, I highly recommend you still enjoy this concrete action, as it can make the movement of the planets more tangible and hardwired in your felt sense. Here are two methods, or you can invent your own. Put your chart on a corkboard and put symbols for the planets on tacks that you then can move around the outside edge of your chart. Or draw your chart on a dedicated whiteboard, and take a moment each week to draw the planets where they are that day. Just drawing your chart helps imprint on your nervous system the unique pattern of your relationship to the planets in a way that merely looking at it never quite does. Find a way to notice where the planets are moving on a regular basis and how they move through your chart. Let the planets teach you.

However you approach it, whether electronically or mechanically, begin to notice where the Moon is in your chart every few days. That Moon will sweep through your charts once a month and conjunct, trine, oppose, square, and sextile each of your natal planets.

The Moon through the signs changes the atmosphere of our emotional and environmental milieu. It sets the tone for the day. Watch the changes in any crowd. How people dress on the subway, how they handle minor inconveniences, and their daily habits all speak of the sign of the Moon at that moment. Let your observations of your own mood and the world around you teach you about your unique relationship to the nature of the signs.

As you watch the Moon go through the signs each month, forming all those aspects to your natal chart, you learn how you respond to planets in that sign, in that house, playing those chords of your natal chart. Every month that transiting Moon will hit a slightly different note because the Sun and all the other planets have now changed places, but you can begin to feel the pattern of your unique responses to the Moon moving through the signs and the houses of your chart.

Through this next month, make a note of your response as the Moon changes signs and moves through the houses of your chart. Note how you respond, what you sense about the feeling of the world, your moods, your appetite, your dreams, your attitude, and the attitude of people around you. Next month, on the same cycle, notice how you feel as that Moon conjuncts each of your planets as it goes around the chart, enlivening them for those 12 hours.

Once you know how you respond to the Moon in Scorpio—opposing your Venus, for instance—you have a map for how you will respond when other planets do the same.

Each transiting planet brings a different message. The transiting planet can act like an action verb on the planet it activates and gives it a new action plan. That action depends on the nature of the planets and the nature of the aspects. To understand that nature, go back and read about the gift, the practical side, and the challenge of that planet and aspect, and read the prompts below. While you will feel the gift edge of the aspects more often under a positive transit, for instance, a trine, conjunction, or sextile, that potential is still there under the tough aspects, though it could be less comfortable. Conversely, when you are under those easy, supportive aspects from a transiting planet, be aware of the potential for that challenging edge, as that may be the spur to push you to grow.

You can feel a planet approaching, the strength of the aspect grows and applies pressure until it perfects or becomes exact. Then as the aspect separates, the nature of the aspect shifts, still with lingering residual effects but with less pressure. Events often occur in our lives not at the peak of the aspect, but in an overlap of several transits at the same time. A fast-moving Moon conjunct to your ascendant can trigger a minor moodiness on an ordinary month. However, it can also facilitate meeting a new friend when transiting Venus approaches your natal Mars and transiting Jupiter approaches your natal Venus.

The Sun illuminates and energizes whatever planet it touches in your chart. It will only last for a few days, never retrograde back, but can help you see and understand the meaning of those points in your chart as it passes by every year.

Every year the Sun goes around your chart, through all the houses, and conjuncts all your planets. These transits occur once every year and signify your yearly cycles. When the transiting Sun conjuncts and enlivens your natal Mars as transiting, Mars conjuncts transiting Uranus, and those two transit your ascendant, you might find yourself in an argument or an accident unless you are carefully building a wall or confronting a perpetrator in court, or have another clear place to put this rather explosive and physical energy.

Look at your chart and notice how the Sun progresses through your houses, and how it lights up your planets once a year. Notice if you have any regular yearly cycles of health or retreat, engagement or hard work, and how these cycles might align to the transits of the Sun through your houses. Let the Sun teach you about the nature of your houses.

Transits from the Wandering Planets

All the planets but the Sun and Moon occasionally turn retrograde, and you will feel that transit three times: when it first forms the aspect, a second time when it retrogrades over it, and a third time when it crosses it again. Sometimes, with the outer planets, those retrograde cycles overlap and the aspect can perseverate. In this case, the first pass usually brings up the problem, gift, or situation, or the story of that transit, the second retrograde pass asks you to work it, and the third pass brings some form of resolution.

Let's look at an example from my practice. A client came to me at a tough turning point as transiting Saturn (Saturn as the action verb) squared his natal Saturn (structure)-Uranus (change)-conjunction. I asked him if he was having trouble changing gears, a symbolic image for that transit. He admitted yes, his life was in an upheaval because his difficulties adapting to change at work had just lost him a job. His knees (bones are ruled by Saturn) hurt, which made it hard for him to climb or move around quickly. And when he left my office, his car wouldn't start because the transmission had blown. Quite literally, he could not change gears. All these issues illustrated challenges around structure, advancement, and change—all Saturn-Uranus questions. Once he grasped this symbolic pattern and accepted that he had stubbornly not been taking care of his structural Saturn issues in his car, body, and personal authority, he chose to adapt—a gift from change-master Uranus—and take responsibility, a gift from Saturn. He started his own business and started claiming his personal authority instead of bucking everybody else's. He fixed his car and knee. Now he could climb, both metaphorically and physically. He began to constellate, to work with, his stars and created a successful life.

Transits by Aspect

Conjunction: When a transiting planet conjuncts one of your natal planets, it infuses its energy into that place. With the conjunction by transit, change comes from within you. Your inner need, drives, compulsion, and growth change, and so changes your life. It shines its light through that planet and gives it more strength. What that means depends on how that planet plays well with others in your natal chart. If the Sun is shining through your Venus, you may be particularly warmhearted and creative for a few days. You may engage in acts of generosity and compassion, but as always, that is up to your natal chart and the choices you make. When Uranus conjuncts your Mars, it nudges you to be an active (Mars) agent of change (Uranus) on and off for about eight months. You can create contrary chaos just because, run away from home and join the circus, resist change, and find yourself accident prone, or be the activist who instigates a change in legislation.

Trine and sextile, when a transiting planet forms a supportive action to your chart, other than a conjunction, it can stimulate your growth by opening doors, creating possibilities in your environment. They do not insist that you pick those up. That is up to you. When Venus trines your Moon, as it does twice a year for a few days, it can soften other harsher aspects. It can lend you a moment of graciousness or just help you find a good deal on something beautiful at the store.

Oppositions: These stimulate your chart through that oppositional energy. That planet in your chart is stimulated by a confrontation from the outside, by an external blockade or active directional force. You are arm-wrestling with those planetary energies. It can be tempting to press fate and prove that you will not be stopped by that blockade, but it may be easier to look at the training and choose carefully which fights you want, and whether that knowledge is actually a call for you to change directions.

Squares: When a transiting planet squares off with one of your natal planets, it can feel like a wrestling match. The effect may be harder to see than opposition because it's coming sideways and stimulates that planet to grow through an often-unexpected challenge. Develop the muscles of that natal planet. It can feel like the universe is tossing you a hot potato and saying, "Here, catch"—a time-sensitive challenge that you would not expect, didn't necessarily ask for and may not have much choice about accepting, but can help you grow in just the way you need.

Inconjunct and semi-sextile: When a planet forms either a 150-degree aspect or a 30-degree aspect to one of your natal planets, it is speaking to that planet from a sign that it has nothing in common with, no polarity, the modality, no element. This aspect can be irritating because it's uncomfortable, but it pushes us to expand our preconceptions and grow. Usually this brings an experience that can feel like a non sequitur, a minor irritation, confusion, or distraction that can act like the grain of sand itching the oyster and causing a pearl to grow.

Here's an example from my own life that illustrates transits at work. Once upon a time, decades ago, I was living with my young family in a small tenement apartment, which we had rehabbed. The rent was so cheap, we could not imagine moving out, even though our family was rapidly outgrowing that space. Transiting Uranus (the changemaker) squared my natal Moon (home, family, daily habits, and life), and it was time to move, but I still could not see how. One week, the ceiling fell in in the hallway, the pipes began to break, and the landlord sold the building to an investor who doubled the price. The universe had made it very clear. We found a place that still needed rehabbing, changing home both by where we lived and the condition of the house we lived within, changed my parenting skills (Moon) as I wrangled toddlers in a construction zone, and, in the long run, created a much better place for our family to grow.

TRANSITS FROM THE PLANETS

Read your transits in reverse order from the Sun. The slower transits form the deeper background settings. A quick Mars transit by itself can mean nothing but a little irritation, where a quick Mars transit while you are in the heart of a Pluto transit can trigger an intense situation that needs you to stay awake, aware, and balanced.

Pluto sets the deep staging, like the bass notes in a piece of music. Neptune creates the atmosphere, talks about the soul hungers and magical elements. Uranus stirs change and transformation. Saturn points out the lessons learned, the disciplines necessary, and Jupiter calls you to expand. Mars is the action planet; Venus brings in heart and art; Mercury, Sun, and Moon bring in the quick-moving interpersonal plotlines.

Pluto Transits

Pluto is so small that you will only feel the transit within a few degrees, but those few degrees will last a couple of years. Since Pluto takes 248 years around the zodiac, you never experience the same Pluto transit twice. Pluto will only transit a portion of your chart during your lifetime. I've sat with many an old person and looked back on their life to study transits. Those elders can usually remember what was going on during challenging Pluto transits and often report that the best and most successful times in their life occurred shortly after a Pluto transit. They often described an experience as if they'd let go of what was unnecessary, resorted their priorities, and watched new life blossom. Some likened a difficult Pluto transit to a forest fire, others as if the stage lights dimmed for a few years. America had just finished its very first Pluto return when Pluto came back to where it was when America was born.

Supportive transits from Pluto help us dive deep. It's a good aspect to do research, investigate, and search for what's missing. We need time alone on retreat. A gentle ache can bring up memories of people, places, and things that we've released in the past and remind us to be grateful. Or it can ask us to let go of what was once appropriate in our lives but no longer fits. We may need to gently release people, places, or things that are not part of the next phase of our life. We need to feel that the people, places, and things in our life matter in the face of life and death. We can dig out jewels from the past and look inside to find new resources. It is a good aspect for exploring psychotherapy, personal development, or finding the gumption to take on a challenge.

Challenging transits from Pluto can whisper a story of mortality and open the door to your psychic basement, and you choose how you respond. You do not need to die, you do not even have to be sick or in danger, but some event or someone near you could be affected. You could realize you drove by an intersection yesterday where there was a fatal accident today. Something could ask you to be fully alive in the face of life or death. Pluto doesn't want you to get depressed, but it is willing to use that as a tool to nudge you out of your comfort zone and into growth. You may feel a loss, loneliness, obsession, or a whiff of depression, or struggle with power and feel a tug-of-war wills. Practically, keep an eye out for basement or sewage problems or dishonest people.

When Pluto talks in your chart, go investigate. Find something to concentrate on. Write down memories that percolate to the surface. Listen to the soul's concerns, but don't get stuck there. Find something worth living for. Pluto asks you who you are in the face of life and death, and it is not a rhetorical question; come up with a good answer, help one other being, and Pluto begins to empower you.

Neptune Transits

Neptune takes about 165 years around the zodiac, about 13 years in a sign, and you feel a Neptune transit for 5 degrees applying, and a few degrees separating, which gives you about two and a half years through a Neptune transit. When Neptune's talking to your chart, it asks you to notice what your soul is hungry for. And it may question your whole concept of reality. Neptune's continuum starts with the positive end of spirituality, intuition, imagination, and feeling at one with the whole. The practical forms of Neptune include water, liquid, oil, weather, and things that flow, with the challenging aspects being illusion, delusion, escapism, alcoholism, or addiction.

Supportive transits from Neptune help you tap into your dream world and become sensitive to your creative Muse. Your barriers grow thin, and you become more permeable. You are invited by Neptune to become more intuitive and compassionate and may find it easier to connect to meditation and prayer. Because your imagination is open and flowing, it may be easier to share your dreams with others. Just remember that not everyone can see what you can see during this transit. It may seem like you're visiting the future, but remember, you still need to manifest those dreams.

Challenging transits from Neptune can stir your escapist edges or leave you confused. Suddenly, the fog rolls in and you can't quite see where you are going. You may have trouble telling the difference between your hopes, fears, and intuition; they all blend together. Water or liquids can become problematic—a cup of tea spills onto the keyboard, a basement floods. You may need more sleep and time in the dream world. You could feel so sensitive that you drift and dream, imagining what would happen if you won the lottery or if your crush called you to go to the ball, and find yourself living in a fantasy instead of using your fantasy to enrich your life. Your favorite form of escape, whether that is extra sleep, fantasy novels, travel brochures, alcohol, or drugs, can beckon to you. Neptune can call for Spirit or spirits.

When Neptune talks to your chart, pretend you are walking in the fog. You can only see what is near you, but you will see it clearly and focus on the present. Neptune transits can help you see this precious moment as sacred and beautiful. But if you look too far ahead into the future, or too far behind into the past, all you'll see is your illusions, delusions, and projections, not reality. Let the past become foggier, be humble about predicting the future, and stay here in the moment when Neptune can work its magic. Envision a lovely next step and then back it up with work. During this transit you also need to consciously give Neptune its due. Take a moment to rest and dream consciously. Meditate or pray long enough to feel connected to Spirit.

If you find Neptune aspects in your natal chart and transits from Neptune tend to bring a hunger for Spirit and magic, which can leave you unusually escapist, you can engage positive Neptune to fill that gap. Many people find the cure for alcoholism, which is a challenging form of Neptune, in a group experience like AA meetings, where when you can psychically soak up (Neptune lends psychic permeability) hope, compassion, and determination for the next step of sobriety, along with a new relationship to the God of your personal understanding, another powerful gift from Neptune.

Uranus Transits

Uranus, God of primordial procreative chaos, is our cosmic clutch. It helps us change, let go of an old gear, and try a new one. Uranus speaks of change, electricity, excitement, genius, and that which is erratic and chaotic. Uranus spends about seven years in a sign. You feel a Uranus transit for months ahead of time. Though it fades fairly quickly, the total transit lasts between approximately nine and 18 months. Expect the unexpected; remember the old phrase from Monty Python, "And now for something completely different."

Supportive transits from Uranus inspire. You probably feel a restlessness growing in your life, particularly around the area represented your natal planet. This aspect can help you let go of what is safe and familiar and try something new. Check out a new piece of technology, consider moving around the world or learning a new language, like French or astrology. Just be careful to be specific about what you need to change. If Uranus trines your Venus, you may need to learn new relationship skills, see one another with fresh eyes, and fall in love again, rather than toss out an old relationship and find a new one that sparkles with that luminous first-love light. If you try to stay in the same old relationship without any changes, you leave yourself open to flame up like a sheaf of wheat when the spark floats by. Find a positive way to bring in a fresh perspective.

Challenging transits from Uranus can make you restless, anxious, and irritable. You can throw the baby out with the bathwater or make a change for change's sake only—and it may not be an improvement. If you resist change because it makes you to uncomfortable, the world around you can help you by breaking down the old and insisting you reach for a new approach.

When Uranus talks in your chart, consider all your options. Take a walk down a road you've never seen. Take a trip or retreat and come back to look at your life with fresh eyes to see what is essential to change and what you can leave alone. Start by changing the habits, and then if you need, change the relationship, move to Madagascar, or challenge yourself in some wildly unusual way. The stronger the Uranus transit, the more important it is for you to figure out what is essential to change and work with, because if you are not in charge of that transformation, it can feel forced upon you. Work with Uranus and evolve.

Saturn Transits

Saturn asks you to grow up. Seen as Father Time or Mother Crone, Saturn symbolizes boundaries, structure, training, mastery learned over time, traditions, bones, teeth, maturity, limitations, authority, policing, and prisons. Saturn takes about two and half years in the sign. You feel Saturn aspects for about nine months.

Supportive transits from Saturn inspire security and structure. They help you tap into your adult self and learn from the teachers around you and the teacher within you. You can more easily organize your thoughts and your desk, tap into tradition, and buckle down to a task that takes concentration. It's a good time to check on the health of your teeth and bones, to assess how you are doing in your work, ask for a raise, or choose to step into the next level of your personal authority.

Challenging transits from Saturn can make you feel like the grown up in the room—cranky, tired, authoritarian, stuck, old, creaky, stiff, brittle, humorless—and all this can leave you depressed. Or maybe you have to deal with someone who is acting like this. Saturn is a martial arts teacher. You may be challenged during this time, just as you would if you were going for the next belt in your martial arts training, when everyone jumps on you at the same time. This is an act of faith from your teacher that you are ready to do this, and when you pass the test, both of you know you earned it, and so does everybody else in the room. You will feel much younger when the aspect has shifted but may notice that you learned important hard lessons during this time and now have more confidence.

When Saturn is talking to your chart, get organized. Tap into something you know well, do what you're good at doing, and the depression eases. Saturn can add strength, but it furthers to stretch your body and mind to regain limberness. And most importantly, look at your life as if this is the teacher you asked for. Figure out what you are here to learn, grow, develop, and strengthen, and do so.

Jupiter Transits

Jupiter is the God who thought he ruled everything. This planet inspires us to think big and symbolizes how we expand our world—through education, law, philosophy, travel, abundance, indulgence, expansive spirit, and a broader perspective. Jupiter spends about a year in a sign, but it is so big, we feel it for a few more degrees. A Jupiter transit lasts between three to nine months.

Supportive transits between the Moon and Jupiter inspire generosity, abundance, optimism, and a philosophical ability to stand back and work for the good of the whole. You may feel a sudden need for freedom and more room to move. You could also eat too much or overdo anything you dive into; choose carefully how you want to expand. It's a good time to ask for a raise or grant, to be generous or encourage the generosity of others. Give hugs, love, and support to one another. It's also a good time to publish, promote, or launch any project that needs visibility, goodwill, or a large audience.

Challenging transits from Jupiter can encourage you to overdo or overindulge, to trust too much, spend too much, give too much, or promise too much. It can also lead to enabling behavior, a tendency to do so much for another that you disempower them and encourage bad behavior. Let these transits challenge you to expand your world in a balanced and farsighted way.

If Jupiter is talking to your chart, stand back and get a more philosophical or global perspective. Ponder the nature of generosity and ask what is real growth and what is the *illusion* of growth. What is a real kindness you can do for others, and what is enabling behavior? Encourage your generous heart, keep a balance, and help all involved (yourself included) feel healthy, satisfied, and empowered.

Mars Transits

Mars, God of all things macho, symbolizes our energy or chi, our strength, entrepreneurial qualities, sexuality, our ability to set boundaries and regulate our immune system, the military, temper, explosions, and accidents. A

Mars transit can last between one month and six months, depending on where you catch it in its retrograde cycle. **Supportive transits from Mars** lend strength, machismo, and protectiveness. Mars is an action verb and wants you to move. It can help you lift rocks, move a piano, spark passion, or help you establish clear boundaries and clarify what you want and need. Your "yes" can be clear if your "no" can truly mean no. Mars can loan you gumption. Just be careful not to run roughshod over people who are not in the middle of their Mars transit.

Challenging transits from Mars can bring out irritability, willfulness, anger, aggression, or inspire a belligerent, competitive, or contrary attitude. Under a Mars square, you can debate even simple household chores. You can become more easily frustrated and can get distracted and therefore careless. Accidents increase under Mars transit when you are thinking about what you want to do or how you want to tell someone off and are not paying attention to the moment. If you stay present with even a tough Mars aspect, you may be more present, more physically skilled, and therefore safer. Pay attention.

When Mars transits talk to your chart, you may feel twitchy or ready for a fight. Go get physical; exercise or chop wood, scrub a floor, or take a brisk walk and then come back and finesse that argument. If you suddenly feel accident prone while cooking breakfast, step away for a minute. Acknowledge what you want or what upsets you, if only to yourself, and you'll feel safer carrying that coffee cup or slicing that bagel. Mars brings out your inner adolescent and shortens your patience and impulse control, but it helps you cut through the dross and see clearly what you want and what you do not want. Mars offers you a chance to realign with your inner truth. Look around and see who needs defending, who needs a hero, and stand up for what is right in the world around you. Just notice that under a Mars transit it seems to make more sense to fight than to negotiate, and this may not be the real truth.

Venus Transits

Venus, the gracious muse and queen of matters of the heart and art, symbolizes our creative process, what we love, what we value, and what we find beautiful and delicious. She stays within a few signs of the Sun, travels around the zodiac roughly every year, retrogrades every 18 months, and, unless you are dealing with the Venus-retrograde redo, you will feel a Venus transit for only a few days to a few weeks.

Supportive aspects from Venus warm our hearts and add sociability and compassion. These aspects soften you, loan you charm, and encourage diplomacy and kindness, and so help any work or social situation where you need to encourage the goodwill of others. Venus aspects can help you connect to your senses and feel affectionately sensual. Nice things can look beautiful, and it is so easy to spend money; just make sure you need the item more than you need the money, as Venus does not bring practicality. You can feel more lovable or long to be loved.

Challenging aspects from Venus can bring an awkward spate, and put you out of sync or on edge. One level of Dante's hell was reserved for crimes of the heart, where lovers swirled around in a hot-pink storm, which is how the surface of the planet Venus has been described. Your heart may become less convenient, and either cool off or heat up without warning. You can feel unloved or long for proof that you are lovable when no one else has changed the thing around you. Or it can just give you a bad hair day. You may feel even more demanding or more easily irritated by people who normally make you happy. Your sense of aesthetics may be off, so consider not making semipermanent decisions like hair color or house paint when Venus is challenging your chart. Use this itch to notice the sandpaper of life, what's been really bothering you underneath your graciousness, but see if you can respond by growing the beauty in the world. **When Venus talks to your chart**, instead of moping, this is a good time to reach out, meet new people, help someone less fortunate, or go pet puppies at the pound. Make an offering to Venus with your warmth and watch her speak back to you. If your heart is stirred up, perform a random act of kindness, dig out the art supplies, or sing in the shower. Give those emotions somewhere productive to go. If you are in an awkward social situation, haul out more formal Venus habits and be diplomatic and polite, even when feeling uncomfortable; trust Venus to smooth over rough edges.

Mercury Transits

The messenger, patron saint of the modern world, describes our mental switchboard: how we move, talk, and organize our thinking. It also controls the traffic of our life: how we transport people, things, and ideas. Practical Mercury is expressed through all systems that help people, things, and information get around: the Internet, phone, newspapers, broadcasting, airplanes, cars, trains, and simple conversations. Mercury rotates around the Zodiac approximately once a year and and is always in the same sign as the Sun, the one before, or the one after. Mercury transits can last for days, unless you're at the edge of a retrograde cycle, in which case the transit lasts about six weeks.

Supportive Mercury transits call for your attention. They can loan you speed and consciousness, the ability to think it through and get perspective, and help you bring your mind to any problem and find an answer. They can help you find the words to support swift movement, understanding, divine wisdom, intellect, broadcasting, travel, and communications technology.

Challenging transits from Mercury can amp up the nervous system and bring a tendency to get lost in the mind. A square from Mercury can feel like a quick review of Mercury retrograde and inspire glitches in all things mercurial. We can get more edgy, irritable, anxious, scattered, diffused, glib, and have to deal with theft, dishonesty, rationalization, or an argument between head and heart.

If Mercury is talking to your chart, use the positive expression of Mercury to solve the problem; reconnect your mind and your heart. Mercury may carry the messages of the Gods to you, but for now you may need to talk to the Gods; don't make it a rationalized plea for what you want. Instead ask for true understanding of the situation. Attend your nervous system, take a deep breath, and relax. Encourage your companions to talk and practice listening.

Think back on important times in your life, both difficult experiences and wonderful moments. Notice where the planets were at those moments and how they were talking to your chart. You are your greatest example. You know those transits from the inside out. Let your life teach you about astrology.

CHAPTER 8

CHART OVERVIEW:
SUMMARY AND PRACTICE

I invite you to walk through one chart reading with me to review what you've learned and to practice how these astrological pieces fit together. As we walk through his chart, I'll ask you to review the same points on your chart. Every chart is an amazing unfolding story. We can look at the chart of famous people because their biography is easily available, and any student can read up on them to see how their chart unfolded over time.

This will be a quick overview. A chart is a complex story that you can spend hours and years uncovering. It contains layers of information packed away that you find as you dig in. But it's always good to start with an overview and see how the big pieces fit together.

Here is the chart of Mohandas Gandhi, from Astro.com's
rectified birth data for October 2, 1869, at 07:08:12.

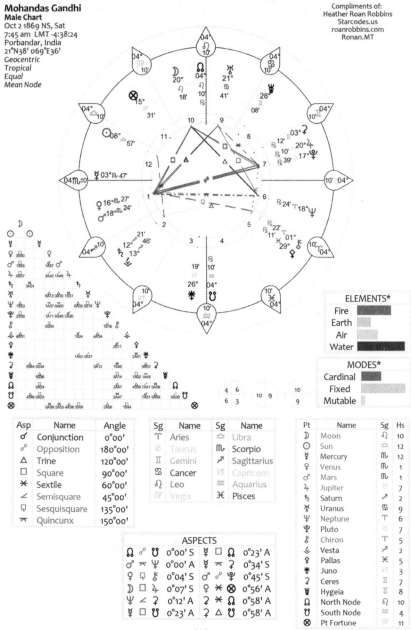

Mohandas Gandhi
Male Chart
Oct 2 1869 NS, Sat
7:45 am LMT -4:38:24
Porbandar, India
21°N38' 069°E36'
Geocentric
Tropical
Equal
Mean Node

Compliments of:
Heather Roan Robbins
Starcodes.us
roanrobbins.com
Ronan.MT

ELEMENTS*

Fire
Earth
Air
Water

MODES*

Cardinal
Fixed
Mutable

Asp	Name	Angle
☌	Conjunction	0°00'
☍	Opposition	180°00'
△	Trine	120°00'
□	Square	90°00'
✳	Sextile	60°00'
∠	Semisquare	45°00'
⬱	Sesquisquare	135°00'
⚻	Quincunx	150°00'

Sg	Name	Sg	Name
♈	Aries	♎	Libra
♉	Taurus	♏	Scorpio
♊	Gemini	♐	Sagittarius
♋	Cancer	♑	Capricorn
♌	Leo	♒	Aquarius
♍	Virgo	♓	Pisces

ASPECTS

☊	☍	☋	0°00' S	☿ □ ☊	0°23' A	
♂	⚻	♆	0°00' A	☿ ⚻ ♃	0°34' S	
♀	⬱	⚷	0°04' S	♂ ☍ ♆	0°45' S	
☽	□	♃	0°07' S	♀ ✳ ⊗	0°56' A	
♆	∠	♃	0°12' A	♃ △ ☋	0°58' A	
☿	□	☋	0°23' A	♃ △ ☋	0°58' A	

Pt	Name	Sg	Hs
☽	Moon	♌	10
☉	Sun	♎	12
☿	Mercury	♏	12
♀	Venus	♏	1
♂	Mars	♏	1
♃	Jupiter	♉	7
♄	Saturn	♐	2
♅	Uranus	♋	9
♆	Neptune	♈	6
♇	Pluto	♉	7
⚷	Chiron	♈	5
⚶	Vesta	♐	2
♀	Pallas	♓	5
⚵	Juno	♑	3
⚳	Ceres	♊	7
⚕	Hygiea	♊	8
☊	North Node	♌	10
☋	South Node	♒	4
⊗	Pt Fortune	♍	11

Mohandas Gandhi was an English-trained lawyer who led India's revolution from the English empire and established its independence, and did so through intelligence, articulation, and charismatic leadership of radical nonviolent protest. He certainly used his powers for the good of the world. He freed his home country of India and set an international model for nonviolent protest and dynamic leadership.

First notice the Sun, Moon, and ascendant. They form the framework or skeleton that holds the rest of the chart. Look to the Sun and house of the luminaries, the Sun and Moon, sources of energy in the chart.

Remember this basic pattern in your chart—where are your Sun, Moon, and ascendant, and how do they relate? How do these three form a framework or skeleton that holds the rest of the chart together?

Gandhi was born just after sunrise with both the Sun and ascendant in peace-loving, social justice–loving Libra. His Sun shone from the twelfth house, the house that illuminates our inner world. Often people with the Sun in the twelfth house feel hidden as a child and become more visible as an adult. They retain the need for a deep inner world and will always need times of privacy, when they can retreat from the world. They can also feel as if their life's work began in another lifetime.

The Sun in the twelfth house and his charismatic Moon in Leo in the tenth house of career points to his highly visible and connected personality, often in the public eye. This visible personality gave him leverage in his world. He was as at home in the public as he was in his private retreats—he needed both, and each venue supported the other, though it was probably a hard balance in the early years.

His Leo Moon also gave him dramatic panache. He knew how to play his part and dress for his role. When he first came to England, he worked hard to fit in, trying to find just the right outfits to do so, until he realized that the best way to become more English than the English was to ignore the dress and instead brilliantly study the law. When he came back to India, he dove into traditional crafts of India, traditional dress of India, and inhabited the role of a wise holy man. With that charismatic Moon in Leo at the top of the chart, when he led a protest, he could gather the crowds.

Gandhi has a paradoxical pattern that pulled on him and created a complexity that enriched his path: the tension between his private Sun in the twelfth house and his so-public Leo Moon in the tenth house. Do you notice any major paradoxes in your chart that make you unique?

Look at the balance between the quadrants in his chart. He balanced both the rich inner life and action out there in the world, both stimulated by his inner calling and in response to the conditions he saw in the world around him.

Review the balance of quadrants in your chart—are you strong in the first quadrant of self-sufficiency and personal exploration, the second quadrant of personal relationships, the third quadrant of interpersonal exploration, or the fourth quadrant integration and maturation?

His chart is high in fire and water. It is an emotionally based chart, but it is lower in the element air; although he was eloquent, he made his point through action even more than words. His chart is lowest on Earth, so practicality was not his driving force, but he did choose grounding habits by walking on the Earth, eating simple vegetarian food, and spinning cotton as a way of invoking Earth to balance his life, stabilize his nervous system, and offer a pragmatic example of his philosophies.

His chart is strong and cardinal, strongest in fixed signs and weak in mutable. His ability to follow through on what he said he would do was his superpower. When he said he was going to fast, he did so without fail. When he said he'd bring a group together and take them on a march, he followed through and brought the crowds. Although he adapted to new situations and times in his life, I don't think anyone would have called him flexible. He was the solid center post for the movement to free India.

Elements and modalities: Review your chart and see which elements are strong in your chart and which are weak. Have you found a way to bring in those missing elements through the charts of people you know or the actions you choose? Notice the balance between cardinal, fixed, and mutable in your chart and ponder how this reflects your love of beginning, of follow-through, or of explaining and translating concepts.

Gandhi has his Sun in the cardinal air sign Libra, the sign that longs for social justice and order, for fairness and beauty. Librans can sometimes delicately skim the surface, but his Mercury, Venus, and Mars in Scorpio all wanted to understand, go deep, and look at the very toughest elements. Venus rules his Sun and his ascendant, so it is considered the ruler of the chart, although Venus is in its detriment, Scorpio, the sign opposite Venus's ruler Taurus. It's conjunct is Mars, powerful in its own sign of Scorpio. Venus and Mars are both out of sect; they are planets comfortable in the nighttime but are in a daytime chart, and so they did not operate like a normal romantic and attractive Venus-and-Mars conjunction.

What planet rules the sign on your ascendant and the sign of your Sun? What is the condition of these planets? Are they in sect, in the time of day they like? Do these two planets get along by sign and aspect? Are they strong or challenged by their sign? Remember this does not make you a good or bad person, nor with a good or bad life, but it can help you understand where the energy flows in your life and where it takes more consciousness and effort.

Venus and Mars conjunct in Scorpio add to his powerful personality. They add primal charisma, focus, resilience, and endurance, and a tendency to keep his own feelings close to his chest. Scorpio can be extreme about emotional and sexual energy, though not always conscious or aware of it. His intimate life is one place where his story and his philosophy could be at odds. He was a great proponent of the emancipation and support for women but did not always act as such in his personal life. He was a proponent of abstinence to grow his personal focus but seemed to surround himself with beautiful women.

Scorpio energy can bring extremes, but in any direction, how we use that Scorpio focus is our choice. The symbol for Scorpio is both the eagle and the scorpion, the highest and lowest perspectives. It can look for all answers within sexuality, or it can focus control into intense abstinence. Gandhi also fasted frequently, both for his own health and, in extremes, as a protest, another disciplined approach to bodily appetites. Scorpio likes to be in control of its extremes.

How do your Sun and Moon get along, and how did your Venus and Mars get along? Are they in comfortable signs? Which planet is stronger by placement? Did you see healthy and easy relationships modeled for you as a child, or challenging ones? And do you see this reflected in your Sun and Moon, Venus and Mars? If they are challenged, you may have had extra work to conceive of how your inner male and female can get along. You may also struggle to negotiate for your needs, but when you do, you have layers of understanding and empathy that someone whose emotional world appears easier may not have.

The only aspect his private, social justice–loving Sun makes is a supportive sextile to serious Saturn in the second house of material resources. Saturn in the second house can bring a sense of restriction, if a stable one, to finances and resources. It can mean inherited money, working hard for one's money, money through traditions and history, and tends to bring financial discipline. He chose poverty in the latter part of his life and put the donations he received into a trust for public needs, and spun cotton as a symbol of the basic daily work that he thought would bring India back to its identity and independence.

Saturn forms a grand trine in fire signs, a real empowering, momentum-building aspect, with his public Leo Moon and Neptune in the sixth house. He was public about his chosen poverty, and he did it with a sense of spiritual and philosophic purpose, as a service to the cause, represented by that Neptune in the sixth house.

What planets aspect your Sun, and how do you see those planets affecting your basic personality?

The highest planet in his chart is Uranus, so his call was not to accept the status quo but to facilitate change, transformation, and adaptation in his world.

What planet is highest in your chart? Closest to the midheaven? If there are no planets above the horizon, what planet rules you midheaven? How do you see this as your spokesplanet, a point that helps you communicate to the world and be visible in the public eye?

He has a focused T-square created on one corner with Venus and Mars conjunct in Scorpio in the first house. Both are opposed to Jupiter and Pluto on another corner in the seventh house of equal others, and all four of these planets square his Moon in Leo.

That seventh house can represent the powerbrokers he had to deal with, both the empowered people working with him for the freedom of India and the powers he challenged, the British Empire itself. That powerful double-opposition square of his Moon in Leo at the top of the chart builds a dynamic combustion engine. A T-square can create a parabolic mirror that focuses its energy on the missing corner of the square. The missing corner of the square in his chart would be about 19 degrees of Aquarius in the fourth house. One way of describing that point would be the Aquarius collective community, the masses that he led in huge protests concerning the rights of the homeland and home rule—the fourth house—for his country of India.

Do you have a minor or major pattern that stands out to you as the strongest in your chart? How did the planets involved in this pattern, several planets in a relationship together, describe some key elements of your own life?

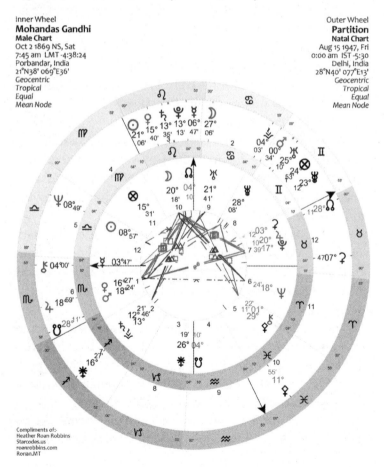

Inner Wheel
Mohandas Gandhi
Male Chart
Oct 2 1869 NS, Sat
7:45 am LMT -4:38:24
Porbandar, India
21°N38' 069°E36'
Geocentric
Tropical
Equal
Mean Node

Outer Wheel
Partition
Natal Chart
Aug 15 1947, Fri
0:00 am IST -5:30
Delhi, India
28°N40' 077°E13'
Geocentric
Tropical
Equal
Mean Node

Compliments of:-
Heather Roan Robbins
Starcodes.us
roanrobbins.com
Ronan.MT

Here is Gandhi's chart on the inside with the transits for the official day of India's independence on the outer ring. This is also the day of the partition between India and Pakistan, dividing the Hindu and Muslim countries. India's independence from England was Gandhi's lifelong wish and work. He poured everything he had into it. But he dearly wanted his country to stay whole. He wanted the Hindus and the Muslims to work together and create one wonderful country. This didn't work, so his greatest joy, India's independence, and his worst fear, the partition, occurred at the same time. He was killed soon after by a Hindu fanatic, one of his own people, for insisting that the Hindus and Muslims reconcile.

Notice transiting Neptune exactly conjuncts his Sun. This day was both the realization of his Neptunian vision and a terrible confusion about purpose and costs going forward. Chiron, the asteroid associated with the archetype of the wounded healer, conjuncts his Mercury, his thinking process. He saw the pain of the countries division. Jupiter had just conjuncted his Venus and Mars, during the final stages of Indian independence, bringing a huge emotional upswelling and high visibility. Jupiter magnifies whatever it touches. Notice the stellium of five transiting planets running together in Leo in his house of professional calling, and right near his Moon. At the stroke of midnight, when the treaty came into effect, the transiting Moon was conjunct his natal midheaven, his most public place. The Moon goes to the chart every month, conjuncting each point every month. By itself, the lunar aspect just means an inclination, but it can act like a trigger when there are bigger, slower transits by the outer planets in play at the time. He certainly was the Leonine center of attention for this process in all its complexities. Venus, the Sun, and Mercury in Leo shone light on his ideals. Saturn conjunct Pluto speaks of the power and the power struggles involved. India and Pakistan were now empowered to be on their own, but the process of partition killed hundreds of thousands of people.

We could go on forever. A chart packs an amazing amount of information; this is but a sketch. Feel free to take this chart and do your own research on Gandhi and that moment of independence to learn more about how astrology and its cycles unfold.

THE NEXT STEP

Practice and explore. Take the charts of people you know and love, people you can ask questions to, and humbly peer within. Instead of telling your friends who they are or what they are like by looking at their charts, consider developing an idea of what they are like or what might've happened and asking them if this is so. Let them teach you about all the many ways these symbols can unfold. Always allow room for the gift of free will and choice, for Spirit, and for guidance. Consider starting a study group in your area to compare charts and learn from one another's life stories.

May the stars be with you.

GLOSSARY

A

Afflicted: Challenging planetary aspects or placements. Squares, oppositions, quincunx, semi-squares, semi-sextiles. In a natal chart, under the "whatever doesn't kill you makes you stronger" theory, learning to integrate and grow from afflicted aspects often develops the soul and forms the drive for the chart.

Alpheta: A term used in traditional astrology meaning "giver of life," it is a planet or point that most supports the life force of the chart and can act as a trigger for health issues.

Almuten: The Almuten system is one method used to compare the relative dignity and ability of all the planets in the search for the overall strongest ruling planet. A planet in the sign that it rules is given +5 points, in exaltation +4, triplicity +3, term +2, and face +1.

Aneretic degree: This is the last degree of the sign, 29°, a degree which can either hold a crisis of identity between the nature of the two signs or form a bridge and incorporate the best of both signs. This degree often implies the end of the cycle, a chapter review of the lessons of that sign.

Angles: a.k.a. cardinal points. Like tent pegs that hold up the tent, these four points form the structure of a chart, and how that chart connects to the Earth and to your world. The angles are the ascendant and descendant, where the Sun goes above and below the horizon, and the midheaven and the IC, formed by your relationship to the center of the Earth and the zodiac above.

Aphelion: The point in a planet's orbit when it is farthest from the Sun as seen from the Earth. At this point it may appear to move slower and may have slightly less influence.

Aphesis: A Greek word for *release*. Used in system of astrological timing—as if the planets are running a relay race—when one particular phase is over, the rulership of the incoming phase is released to the next ruler, like the passing of the torch.

Apogee: The point in a planet's orbit when it is its farthest from the Earth. Here the planet appears smaller and feels farther away.

Apparent motion: Earthlings see things from our own perspective, but we are not the center of our solar system. We perceive the motion of the other planets in the solar system from our off-center vantage point; this complicated pattern is psychologically relevant even if it's not astronomically correct. For example: the Sun and planets appear to travel from the east to the west each day because our Earth is turning in the opposite direction. The signs of the zodiac appear to rise at the ascendant and set in the West, but in reality, they do not move. Instead the Earth rotates. No planet actually goes backward, but because of the difference in the speed of our orbit and theirs, and their relative position to the Sun compared to ours, a planet can appear to back up or turn retrograde.

Application/applying aspects: A faster-moving planet is approaching—or applying to—an aspect with a slower moving planet. An applying aspect will be more intense in the days or hours to come as it has not yet peaked; because it is waxing rather than waning, it generally has more strength and implies a story to come when the aspect perfects.

Arabic parts: Also known as Arabic lots, an extensive pre-Hellenistic method which creates points based on mathematical calculations that act as an important trigger in the chart; the distance between two points is added or subtracted to a third to derive the location of the lot, and the formula changes if the chart is a daytime or nighttime chart. The most common use part is the part of fortune, which can act like a mini-Jupiter. For a daytime chart, start with the degree of the ascendant, add the degree of the Moon, then subtract the degree of the Sun. For the nighttime chart, start with the ascendant and add the degrees of the Sun then subtract the degrees of the Moon. Or let a computer do it for you. The fact that these lots work is another example of the amazing web of interconnected rhythm and pattern in the universe.

Arc: A part of a circle. Astrologers measure the distance between two planets or points and use this as a unit of measurement. For example, the Solar arc describes the distance the Sun travels during a specific time, which is then used to move all the other planets the same distance and notice their new relationship. This is another example of the strange rhythms we notice in astrology; it may not be clear how it works, but is a powerful tool.

Ascendant: Also known as the rising sign, or the degree of the zodiac just coming up over the eastern horizon at the birthplace and time. The ascendant describes the doorway through which you see the world and the world sees you.

Asteroids: Astrologers use the larger asteroids in and around our solar system to add detail and breadth. Sketch in the basics of the chart, then add the asteroids; like sketching a face, you want to make sure the eyes, ears, and mouth are in proportion before you add eyebrows and freckles. The most commonly used asteroids are in the asteroid belt between Mars and Jupiter, which appears to be a planet that never quite formed because of Jupiter's enormous gravitational field. Chiron, the asteroid between Saturn and Uranus, is considered a bridge between the traditional planets and the outer ones.

Aspect: A geometrical relationship between two celestial points or planets, this pattern describes the nature of their relationship, the energy that flows between them.

Aversion: This term is used for minor difficult aspects, the semi-sextile and the quincunx, which describe a relationship between signs of the zodiac that have nothing in common, no modality, no polarity, and no element. Because these planets have nothing in common, they relate uncomfortably, but, just like a good conversation with a stranger, we can grow when we stretch ourselves and consciously create connection.

B

Barren signs: Gemini, Leo, and Virgo are considered barren, signs that are not fertile and are focused on harvesting, weeding, tilling, thinking, or being, rather than nurturing offspring. Planets in the signs can help us be great with children but are seen as more mentors than cuddly nurturers.

Benefics: Jupiter and Venus are generally considered the bountiful, beneficent planets, though each has a problem in its extreme. Sometimes they bring too much of a bad thing.

Bicorporal signs: Also called double-bodied. The mutable signs whose symbol contain two things relating, Gemini (the twins),

Sagittarius (half-man, half-horse), Pisces (two fishes), and Virgo (a woman holding a sheaf of wheat).

Birth chart: Also known as a natal chart or horoscope, this is the abstracted map of the planets in relationship to the surface of the Earth and the zodiac around the Earth at the moment a soul is born, usually seen as the first breath or first moment outside the mother's womb.

Biquintile: A minor good aspect of 144 degrees.

Bounds: Also known as terms. From the Latin *termini*, which means *bounds* or *edges*, terms divide the signs into smaller parts ruled by different planets in subtle layers. It is a system used in ancient Greek and Egyptian astrology for a minor dignity. The bounds are created by the path of the Sun, from 23 degrees, 27 minutes north to 23 degrees, 27 minutes south of the ecliptic, the part of the sky that describes the zodiac. A planet within this area is within bounds, within expectations. When a planet is out of bounds, when its declination takes it north or south of this band, it is considered out of bounds, a wildcard, and can act think outside of the box and influence with unpredictability, for better or for worse. You could think of a planet in bounds as a person who goes to school, lives in town, and has a good job, and the eccentric artist who travels the world and lives off the grid as out of bounds. We need all approaches.

C

Cadent: The last house of each quarter, a.k.a. the mutable houses, the third, sixth, ninth, and twelfth. Traditionally these were considered weaker houses, and planets there were considered weaker unless they were the natural rulers such as Mercury in the third or sixth, or Jupiter the ninth or twelfth. That attitude has changed with recent astrological research. Michel Gauquelin pointed out that these planets in the cadent houses have just hit the cardinal points and, statistically, have a lot to do with the interests and fate of that person. In my experience, planets in the cadent houses are often hard for the person to express growing up but are driving forces that take the lead in their adult life, particularly planets in the twelfth house within 15 degrees of the ascendant.

Cardinal signs: The signs that begin a season: Aries, Cancer, Libra, Capricorn. Each season begins with a brash, innovative cardinal sign, full of energy to initiate and motivate. In the northern hemisphere, Aries begins spring, Cancer initiates summer, Libra starts autumn, and Capricorn brings in winter. Reverse the seasons for the southern hemisphere.

Cardinal points: The angles of a chart, the ascendant, descendant, midheaven, and IC. The cardinal houses follow after the cardinal points, the first, fourth, seventh, and tenth houses.

Cazimi: Although planets close to the Sun (see combust) are considered weakened or overshadowed by the Sun's dominant energy, Cazimi describes an extremely close conjunction to the Sun, within one degree and strongest if within 16 minutes, called "in the heart," a relationship which merges their energy and adds power to the planet.

Celestial equator: The terrestrial equator, that line equidistant from our poles, extended into space.

Chaldean order: A system used in traditional astrology that lists the seven classical planets in order from the slowest to the fastest as seen here on Earth: Saturn, Jupiter, Mars, Sun, Venus, Mercury, and the Moon.

Combust: Any planet within 15 degrees of the Sun but not cazimi cannot be seen in the sky and is considered combust. The Sun normally strengthens a planet by contact via aspect and can subsume the energy of a planet. That planet flavors or imbues into the Sun's energy. They operate as one unit, but the individual personality of each planet can feel subsumed.

Composite chart: Two, sometimes more, individual charts are merged to form one new chart: the chart of the relationship itself. There are several different methods to form this third chart. Most common is the composite midpoint method, which finds the midpoint between the two Moons, the two Suns, the two ascendants; this chart is read not by sign but by house and aspects, and transits to those points. Those midpoints can act like keys on an autoharp, where a transit to them rings the dynamics between the two people and echoes in their relationship.

Configuration: An aspect that has three or more planets, like a yod, a T-square, a grand trine, or a grand square.

Conjunction: Two planets that work together because they are within 11 degrees if the Sun or Moon is involved, and usually 8 degrees if between two planets. As if they are yoked together, they become a team and can double their pull but are limited in their independence.

Co-significator: Like any village, who rules what can be a matter of complex relationships. There may be a primary ruler, which you talk to or check its transits to understand the influences, and a co-ruler or co-significator, which will also be an influence. For example, the ruler of the sign on the ascendant is considered the significator of the chart, but any planet in the first house is a co-significator. For a specific question, the ruler of the sign on the house cusp would be the significator, the natural ruler of the house, the ruler of the terms, or the ruler of the subject, like the Moon or Venus for relationship questions. Always look to the primary rulership first. Nothing is louder than that influence. Then fill in the information with the other guys. Both traditional astrology and horary astrology have complex pecking orders, which help you sort the signification.

Critical degrees: Also known as sensitive degrees, these are given considerable importance in traditional astrology. Like a baseball base, they are a buzzing, energized place, and a planet's strength increases when it lands here—which is great for the easy planets and challenging for the tough ones. For the cardinal signs, the critical degrees are 0, 13, and 26. For fixed signs the critical degrees are 9 and 21. For the mutable signs, the critical degrees are 4 and 17. Many astrologers consider 0 and 29 degrees of any sign to also be critical degrees.

Containment: A planet is contained by the two planets on either side, like a planetary sandwich. This relationship is more noticeable if they are close together, but we feel this pattern no matter how far apart. The Moon will transit these planets in the same order every month, and the Sun, Venus, and Mercury transit them, in this order, every year and underline this connection.

Chronocrator: From the Greek word *chronos* (time) and *crator* (lord), the chronocrator is the significator and ruler of a particular span of time. Traditional astrology uses several methods to figure out the rhythm and timing in your life, periods of time where planets trade off leadership of your life like a relay race, and generalized timing. In my experience, the time-lord systems set a background, and the play on the stage can be seen through transits and progressions. Who the time lord of a particular time in your life is depends on which system you are using at the moment; an Internet search will provide several calculators.

Cusp: A cusp is a doorway. The cusp between two signs is the last degree of one and the beginning of another. The cusp between two houses is the edge between them, a place that can move between different house systems. In most of the Western house systems, the ascendant, descendant, IC, and MC are the same, but the interstitial house cusps change depending on the mathematics used to define the houses.

Cycle: The time it takes for a planet or aspect to rotate around the zodiac and come back. For example, the Moon cycles through the zodiac once a month, the Sun once a year.

D

Davison composite chart: The Davison composite, or reference place method, a less-used form of composite charts, finds the date halfway between the two birthdates and the place halfway between the two birthplaces and draws a third composite chart from there.

Debility: A planet who does not have its full power because it's in a sign opposite its ruler, a sign opposite its exaltation, or is in a sign so very different in nature. Sometimes a planet in its debility will actually be more cooperative or diverse in its expression than a planet in its strength, but because its expression is unique and not stereotypical, it needs conscious thoughtfulness to find its potential.

Decan or decanate: Each sign is divided into three divisions of 10 degrees, a decanate, which has a ruler, and that ruler becomes a sub-ruler or co-ruler of that part of the sign. The interaction between the ruler of the sign in the ruler of the decan offers a unique flavor to that neighborhood.

Declination: The distance by degrees of a planet north or south of the celestial equator. If two planets are the same degree, both either north or south, they are considered parallel, which has a similar flavor to a conjunction. If they are the same degree north or south but one on either side of the equator, they are considered contra-parallel, which has a similar flavor to an opposition. If a planet is so far north or south that it is out of the normal zodiacal range of the Sun, it's considered out of bounds, a wildcard.

Decile: Or semi-quintile, 36 degrees or one tenth of the circle, a minor favorable aspect.

Degree: Astrologers use 360 degrees to the circle of the zodiac, 30 degrees to each sign, 60 minutes to each degree, and 60 seconds to each minute to locate a point or planet. Think of degrees like the address on a city block: once you know the system, it can help you locate easily where that point is on the block, and what the cross street is.

Descendant: The opposite point from the ascendant, the cusp of the seventh house, and the point where the Sun would be at sunset. If the world is our front door, how we see the world and how the world sees us, the descendant describes how we perceive other people's energy, what we may project upon them or expect them to hold for us, and a place where they enter our lives.

Detriment: When a planet is in the sign opposite the one it rules, it is considered in detriment, or uncomfortable. For instance, Venus rules Taurus and Libra, and therefore is in detriment in Aries and Scorpio.

Dignities: Places where planets are strong, though strong isn't always wonderful. Planets can be dignified accidentally or essentially. Essential dignity describes the planet as joyful because of its position in the zodiac, in a sign it rules or where it's particularly happy. A sign gains accidental dignity by its place in the chart, whether it's close to an angle, swift and direct in motion, not too close to the Sun, or in a helpful aspect to a beneficent planet or fixed star.

Direct in motion: Moving in the order of the signs, from Aries toward Taurus and on through the zodiac. Not retrograde.

Dispositor: Another way to perceive rulership, a planet is disposed by another when it resides in that planet's sign. Venus rules Libra, therefore, if another planet like Mercury is in Libra, Venus disposes it or is its dispositor. You can think of it as a managerial relationship: Mercury would look to Venus as its manager.

Diurnal: During the daytime, when the Sun is above the horizon between the ascendant and descendant. Diurnal planets are more comfortable, and stronger in the chart, during the daytime: Sun, Jupiter, Saturn.

Domicile: We are most comfortable in our own home; a planet is most comfortable in the signs it rules, its domicile.

Draconic chart: A chart created by holding all the planets and nodes in their same relationship with one another, while moving the north node to zero degrees of Aries. The draconic chart can act as an extension of the north node and give us clues to the soul's direction.

Dragon's head and tail: The Moon's nodes, the points where the Moon crosses the ecliptic. The head of the dragon is the north lunar node, where the Moon crosses from the southern hemisphere to the northern on the day you were born. The tail of the dragon, or the south lunar node, is opposite, where the Moon crosses the ecliptic from north to south. Together, they point to a direction of soul growth.

E

Earth signs: Taurus, Virgo, Capricorn

Eclipses: Alignments of the Sun, Moon, and Earth by both position in the zodiac, and by position above or below the equator, in such a way where one of the luminaries is temporarily eclipsed or hidden. These points act like astrological acupuncture and pour activating energy into that point. Like acupuncture they can unstick what has been stuck and so precipitate action. Solar and lunar eclipses follow one another. In a solar eclipse, the Moon blocks our view of the Sun. In a lunar eclipse, the Earth's shadow darkens the Sun. Earth is the only planet where the Moon and the Sun appear to be the same size by quirk of size and distance and so create eclipses.

Ecliptic: Or where the eclipses happen; the belt of the Sun's apparent path around the Earth, though in reality it is described by the path of the Earth around the Sun. We measure the ecliptic by longitude by signs and degrees.

Election: Electional astrology works to find the best time for a specific event, to find times to begin projects, get married, start a garden, or start a business.

Elevated: An elevated planet is higher in the sky than others, closest to the midheaven. A planet that is elevating, rising to where the Sun would be right before noon, is considered growing in strength. The highest planet in the chart can focus the chart and has extra strength within the family of the chart, a strong form of accidental dignity.

Elements: The zodiac is divided into four elements—fire, Earth, air, water—also called the triplicities, because there are three signs in each of the four elements who all share the element and speak the same language.

Ephemeris: The astrological almanac listing zodiacal positions of the planets and other astronomical data as it changes through time (in ephemeral motion means ephemeris). This used to be the big book every astrologer carried with them (and some of us still do!), but now this information is readily available online.

Equal house system: In this system, often useful at extreme northern and southern latitudes, the ascendant is derived by normal methods and the 12 houses that follow start at the same degree, with 30 degrees to each house.

Equator: The great circle around the middle of the Earth, equidistant from the poles and which divides the northern and southern hemispheres, defining the parallel of zero degrees. This circle extended into space is called the celestial equator.

Equinox: The time and day where the Sun crosses the celestial equator, creating days and nights of equal lengths at the equator. The spring equinox defines the beginning of Aries in the Western zodiac, and the fall equinox defines the beginning of Libra.

Exaltation: A planet is exalted in a sign that it is strong, second only to being in its domicile, or the sign rules. The Sun is unusually sunlike in Aries, the Moon is at its coziest in Taurus, Mercury is its most nervy and mercurial in Virgo, Venus is its most receptive and charming in Pisces, Mars is its most ambitious and determined in Capricorn, Jupiter is expansive and nurturing in Cancer, and Saturn is its most fair and involved in social justice in Libra.

F

Face: Faces are a one-sixth division of a sign, five degrees. In traditional astrology each has a ruler, and if a planet is in a comfortable relationship with the ruler of the sign of its face, it puts it into a minor position of dignity.

Fall: When a planet is in the sign opposite of its exaltation, it's in its fall or out of its comfortable milieu. An essential debility second only to it being in the sign opposite the one it rules, the planet may be less strong in the chart but add depth to the person. The Sun is in its fall in Libra, where it can't just shine, but it must always be aware of relationships. The Moon is in its fall in Scorpio, where it is comfortable in the depths. Mercury is in its fall in Pisces, or least quick, but potentially more creative, and thinks in Gestalts. Venus is in its fall in Virgo, where the mind and heart always need to work together. Mars moves into protection rather than accomplishment in Cancer. Jupiter in Capricorn can be confused by its role and create hierarchies, and Saturn in Aries can be dominant.

Familiarity: An old term that implies some relationship between two planets, whether it is by aspect or reception. Buddies.

Feminine planets: Moon, Venus, and Neptune.

Feminine signs: The signs are organized by polarity and rotate every other sign. Traditionally known as feminine, now in our more genderfluid world, they are often referred to as yin signs. All Earth and water signs are receptive, with an introspective nature.

Firdaria, Firdar: One of the time lord systems, this one is attributed to the Persians and is similar to zodiacal releasing. If the person is born during the day, begin with the Sun. If at night, begin with the Moon. In this system, the Sun is chronocrator—time lord—for the first 10 years, Venus for the next 8 years, Mercury for 13 years, the Moon for 9 years, Saturn for 11 years, Mars for 7 years, north node for 3 years, south node for 2 years, and then the system recycles. During the cycle of that chronocrator, this planet has an extra effect on the person; to look at what that means, look to that planet's condition in the natal chart.

Fire signs: Aries, Leo, and Sagittarius.

Fixed houses: The houses in the middle of each quadrant, the second, fifth, eighth, and eleventh houses.

Fixed: Taurus, Leo, Scorpio, and Aquarius are fixed signs, the signs in the heart of each season, when there is no doubt what season we're in. These signs hold the cross-quarter days and loan us their stability and sturdiness.

Fixed stars: Considered opposite to the planets, known as the wanderers, the stars that do not move noticeably against the zodiac are considered fixed. The largest and closest fixed stars have an observed effect on our lives, some beneficent, some malefic, some pragmatic.

Fruitful signs: Cancer, Scorpio, and Pisces are particularly fruitful, and so is Taurus.

G

Geocentric: From the Earth's perspective, describing celestial circumstances with the Earth as the center.

Grand cross: A configuration where four planets square in sequence form two sets of oppositions, and so create the four corners of a square. This aspect is as dynamic as a combustion engine and, like that engine, needs a healthy and clear outlet. This is strongest if all planets are in the same modality: cardinal, fixed, or mutable.

Grand trine: When three planets form the three corners of an equilateral triangle, a pattern strongest when they are all in the same element: fire, earth, air, or water. Harmoniously dynamic.

Great year: The period during which Earth's poles complete the zodiacal circle, or one complete cycle of the equinoxes around the ecliptic (known as an astrological age). Approximately 25,800 years.

H

Hard aspects: "May you integrate all your squares" is an astrological blessing. Hard aspects challenge us to grow. They can act like a martial arts teacher, building strength through insisting we tackle a challenge. Too many hard aspects can be discouraging; too few and a person may not get the chance to build up real strength. Many successful charts have a preponderance of hard aspects, which can leave the owner feeling driven and propelled. Conjunctions with difficult planets are considered hard aspects, as our oppositions, squares, semi-squares, and sesqui-quadrates with any planet. Semi-sextiles and quincunx are more irritating than conflict-creating, but annoyingly call us to grow and stretch ourselves.

Hayz, in hayz: An Arabic term that means the planet is happy, in sect, and in a sign of the same polarity. This is a powerful dignity. A diurnal planet is in the same hemisphere as the Sun in a fire or air sign. A nocturnal planet is in the opposite hemisphere of the Sun in a water or Earth sign.

Heliocentric: Though we usually do natal charts from our place here on Earth, we know the Sun is the center of our solar system and can do a heliocentric chart, a chart from the position of the Sun at the moment you were born. The information is a less personal, more universal chart, a place of soul perspective and purpose. One can also do a chart from the perspective of the center of Mars or any of the other planets to get another layer of information about the expression of that planet in the natal chart.

Hellenistic astrology: This form of traditional astrology was practiced from 2nd century B.C.E. through 6th century C.E., derived in the late Hellenistic period of Greece from earlier Babylonian and Egyptian astrology. In recent decades Hellenistic astrology is having a resurgence and its techniques are being rediscovered.

Herschel: Sir William Herschel discovered the planet Uranus on March 13, 1781, and so Uranus's first name was Herschel. Old astrological text may sometimes refer to this name.

Horary astrology: Ask a question and do a chart for that exact moment and read the results. This divination has its own specific rules but can answer complex questions.

Horoscope: From the Greek for "time observer." Inferences made about a person and their future based on the time and place of their birth.

House: Most forms of astrology divide the chart into 12 houses, but there are many different systems to do so. The equal and whole sign houses that do not require math to set up and were used in traditional astrology are having a resurgence today. Some astrologers feel this leaves out a layer of information given by the mathematically derived house systems of Placidus, Koch, Campanus, Porphyry, and Regiomontanus. Each one has its proponents and has something to offer. Try them out and see what works for you. After reviewing all of them through many hundreds of charts and decades of transits, I use the Koch houses.

Hyleg: "Giver of life"; the luminary (Sun or Moon), planet, or point that most supports the life force of the chart can act as a trigger for health issues. The Sun or Moon is considered hyleg if either is on the ascendant, between 5 degrees above or 25 degrees below the ascendant (the planet that has just risen or is about to rise), or in the same relationship to the midheaven or descendant. If neither Sun nor Moon is in relationship to the angles, then the degree of the ascendant becomes our trigger point. It is important to take care of one's health if the hyleg is having a difficult transit, and it can be a wonderful time to improve the health when the hyleg is experiencing a positive transit.

I

IC or Imum Coeli: The bottom of the chart, the cusp of the fourth house, the north angle, the taproot. If you could have stood at your birth and run a plumb line through your spine and through the center of the Earth and outthe other side, there it is.

Increasing in motion: The planets don't change speed in their orbit around the Sun, but we can see them moving faster against the zodiac from our earthly perspective. When a planet is about to retrograde, it appears to slow down and hold still before it backs up.

Once it turns direct, it begins to pick up apparent speed. A planet in the midpoint between two retrograde cycles appears to move through the zodiac at a relatively fast clip and can work smoothly.

Inferior planets: Not the least bit weak, this term refers to planets whose orbits are closer to the Sun than our Earth: Venus and Mercury.

Ingress: The entrance of a planet into a sign. The Sun's ingress into Aries at the moment of the vernal equinox defines springtime. A chart done for the ingress of the Sun into a season at a particular place to give information about that season ahead. A chart done for the ingress of the season in the capital of the country can give a snapshot of the issue that country will face.

Intercepted: There are no intercepted signs in the equal house systems or whole-sign houses. The other, more mathematically derived house systems often have the beginning of one sign on a house cusp and the end of that sign on the next house cusp, which means somewhere else in the chart two signs are intercepted, or contained within a house and do not have representation on a cusp. A planet contained in an intercepted sign may need to be consciously activated, as they don't have a doorway.

J

Joys: A traditional astrology concept, which says planets are happier or have joy in certain houses and signs because it fits their disposition and gives them a healthy outlet, just like a human in congenial surroundings. Mercury has joy in the first house, the Moon has joy in the third house, Venus has joy in the fifth house, Mars has joy in the sixth, the Sun has joy in the ninth, Jupiter in the eleventh, and Saturn in the twelfth. Because a planet has joy doesn't necessarily mean the person does, as that depends on the rest of the chart and the person's choice of expression, but it does add extra strength to that planet.

L

Lights or luminaries: The Sun and the Moon. All the rest of the planets reflect the light of the Sun.

Long ascension signs: Cancer, Leo, Virgo, Libra, Scorpio, and Sagittarius take more time to ascend across the horizon.

Longitude, celestial: A planet's position measured in terms of signs and degrees from the vernal equinox point of zero degrees of Aries along the celestial ecliptic.

Longitude, geographical: The position of any place east or west, measured on the ecliptic, with zero degrees running through Greenwich, England.

Lunation: The Moon takes 27 days, 7 hours, and 43 minutes to circumnavigate the zodiac and come back to the same place. The phases of the Moon describe the lunar cycle. A lunation chart can be drawn up for the new Moon or full—at a specific place—for information about the month ahead.

M

Malefics: Mars, Saturn, Uranus, and Pluto are considered malefic planets by traditional astrology. They more clearly offer us a challenge. It may be just what we need, but not necessarily what we would pray for.

Masculine planets: The yang planets ("masculine" refers more to the active, dry nature of the planet than its nonexistent gender) are Mars, the Sun, Jupiter, Saturn, and Uranus. Mercury is considered mutable, hermaphroditic, and takes on the characteristics of the planets with which it relates.

Masculine signs: Yang signs. All fire and air signs are considered outward-moving, active signs.

Medium Coeli: Also known as the midheaven or meridian, this is the highest point of the chart, where the Sun would be at noon if you lived on the equator. It describes the most public, visible point of the chart, like the flagpole on top of your personal castle.

Modality: The position in the seasons: cardinal, fixed, or mutable. Cardinal signs begin a season, fixed hold the center of the season, and mutable signs complete a season and translate one season into the other.

Mundane astrology: Mundane means of this Earth, daily, practical. Mundane astrology follows the astrological weather of the moments that affect our daily life, our history, our weather, and our politics.

Mutable: The last sign of each season, as weather shifts back and forth and one season transforms into another. Mutable signs impart that versatility—the ability to adjust, explain, and change. Gemini, Virgo, Sagittarius, and Pisces are mutable signs.

Mutual reception: Two planets that are each in the sign ruled by another; for instance, Mercury in Libra with Venus in Virgo. Mutual reception creates a connection between two planets even when there is no other aspect.

N

Nadir: (see *IC*) The bottom of the chart, the taproot. The cusp of the fourth house or point opposite the midheaven.

Natal chart: Birth chart, a snapshot of the solar system at the moment and from the place of a person's birth.

Nocturnal planets: Planets said to be more comfortable during the night. the Moon, Venus, and Mars are nocturnal planets, in sect in a nighttime chart, and stronger than they are in the daytime chart.

Nodes: The point on the zodiac where a planet crosses from the southern hemisphere into the northern hemisphere is its north node; and from the north to the south, it's the south node. Every planet has nodes, and the most commonly used are the lunar nodes.

Northern signs: The Sun has a northern declination from the beginning of Aries through the end of Virgo.

O

Occidental and oriental: A planet is considered oriental if it rises and sets after the Sun, which would make it visible in the evening sky. A planet is considered occidental when it sets and rises before the Sun. An easy way to figure this out is to turn the chart so that the Sun is on the midheaven and note in which hemisphere the planet falls.

Occultation: From *occult*, which means "to hide." An eclipse is a form of occultation. One planet moves in front of the other and occludes it temporarily.

Opposition: 180 degrees apart, directly opposite on the zodiac, an aspect that can feel like two cars heading into the same intersection from opposite directions, or two horses pulling in opposite directions; tense and confronting, but if the collision is avoided and the attention is directed, it can produce energy to drive evolution forward. A full Moon is in opposition between Sun and Moon.

Orb: The orb of influence of an aspect, meaning how far off the exact point do we still feel a square or trine. Often astrologers give one or two more degrees for an applying aspect, one that is intensifying, versus a separating aspect, or one that has peaked already. Every astrologer has their own preferences, but often the luminaries and Jupiter have an orb up to 10 degrees, and the other planets an orb of 8 degrees—for the major aspects of conjunction, opposition, square, trine, with a few less degrees for the more minor aspects. Asteroids and Pluto have a smaller orb, of 2 or 3 degrees. The tighter the orb, the closer the planets are to an exact aspect, the stronger the quality.

Out of bounds: The bounds are described by the path of the Sun, from 23 degrees and 27 minutes north to 23 degrees and 27 minutes south of the ecliptic, from the Tropic of Cancer to the Tropic of Capricorn. When a planet is out of bounds, it's path has wandered north or south of this band; it becomes a wildcard. The elements it governs can become unpredictable.

P

Parallel: When two planets are equal distance from the equator, either north or south, they are considered parallel and aspect with a benign supportive resonance similar to a conjunction.

Part of fortune, Pars Fortunae: The most commonly utilized of the Arabic parts, or mathematical points. In daytime charts this point is calculated by adding the degrees (on the 360 dial) of the ascendant + the Moon and then subtracting the Sun's position. In nocturnal charts this point is found by adding ascendant + the Sun - the Moon. The part of fortune is considered beneficent, a little Jupiter, a place of fortune that refers to the strength of our health, our bodies, our material resources. See *Arabic parts* for more info.

Partile: An aspect that is close to exact, preferably within one degree.

Perigee: The point of a planet's orbit when that planet is nearest the Earth. It may appear bigger, and its influence feels stronger when it is close, versus apogee, the point where it is farthest away. The cycle is particularly noticeable with Venus; when she is closest to Earth she is huge, beautiful, and fills our heart.

Peregrine: This name is from a Latin word meaning "beyond the borders," or wandering far from home. A planet is peregrine when it has no rulership over its position, no essential dignity. It's not in the sign it rules, not exalted, not in its triplicity, term, or face. Like any wanderer far from home, it has less automatic influence on its surroundings, and less authority, though it can be consciously invited in and included.

Perihelion: The point of a planet's oval orbit where it is closest to the Sun.

Personal planets: We share the outer planets' movements with all the people born in our year, where the personal planets are specific. The Sun, Moon, Mercury, Venus, and Mars move fast enough to create a pattern specific to an individual's personal chart, versus the generational or societal patterns of the planets beyond.

Planetary days and hours: In traditional astrology a planet rules each day as well as each hour of the day and influences what works best at that time, a system that easily made sense when we were all aware of sunrise and sunset more than the clock's time. Sunday is ruled by the Sun, Monday by the Moon, Tuesday by Mars, Wednesday by Mercury, Thursday by Jupiter, Friday by Venus, and Saturday by Saturn. The first hour of each day, starting at sunrise, is governed by the planet of that day, and the ruler of the hours follow in the Chaldean order, from slowest to fastest: Saturn, Jupiter, Mars, the Sun, Venus, Mercury, and the Moon. So if the first hour after sunrise on Wednesday was ruled by Mercury, the next would be the Moon, then Saturn, etc. The Internet easily provides this info if you missed the moment of sunrise; search "calculate planetary hours."

Planetary rulers: Astrological rulership does not mean domination, but a more benign sense of affinity, like that with a teacher, shepherd, governor, and significator: someone who you talk to understand and negotiate with that province. Each sign is ruled by a planet. Each house is ruled by the planet that rules the sign on the cusp. Until the discovery of the telescope, only the visible planets were rulers; the newly discovered Uranus, Neptune, and Pluto are now given spiritual rulership over Aquarius, Pisces, and Scorpio respectively, but for most practical concrete divination, astrologers use the traditional rulers.

Polarity: Whether a sign is yin (all the Earth and water signs) or yang (all the fire and air signs). Yin signs are traditionally called female signs or negative signs, as in receptive, passive, introverted signs. Yang signs are traditionally called masculine or positive signs, as in active, extroverted signs. Signs within the same polarity tend to have an affinity, a similar rhythm and understanding.

Primary directions: Like progressions, this predictive technique used in traditional astrology is based on the premise that our experience of the microcosm of the planetary movements in the first few minutes, hours, weeks, and months of our life imprints on us and creates patterns that will resonate throughout our life. Primary directions correlate each degree that crosses the midheaven (roughly one degree every four minutes) to one year of our life.

Progressions: The planets are always moving through time and space. When a person is born, we take a snapshot of the moment of our first independent breath or action under this theory that we imprint that moment; it is our natal chart. The planets keep moving—we imprint the pattern they make in those first few months after our birth, and those patterns sketch out the big sweeping landscapes of our life, and we live out these patterns, with a lot of choice about how, over the course of our life. There are several ways to read the landscape of our chart expanded through time. Secondary and tertiary progressions are the most common forms. Look under those names for details.

Q

Quadrants: The four quarters in a chart created by the horizon of the Earth crossed by the line between midheaven and IC.

Quincunx: An aspect which is about 150 degrees apart (five signs, or one sign off an opposition). A minor but irritating or motivating aspect that can stretch us to grow. It relates to two points in signs that have nothing in common—no polarity, element, or modality—and so have to learn to communicate.

Quindecile: A minor positive aspect of 24 degrees.

Quintile: A minor positive aspect of 72 degrees, one fifth of the circle, which implies an unusual creative gift or talent.

R

Radix, radical, root: The natal chart is the root to the rest of the work; *radix* refers to the natal chart or to the root chart of an event or question.

Rays: Beams or aspects, conduits of energy that connect planets. Another usage of the term is in esoteric astrology, first introduced by Alice Bailey and supposedly a translation from Tibetan teachings, which describes a system of the seven energetic rays with the planets as their first expression.

Reception: How one planet receives the other, as it might a guest. If Mars is in Venus-ruled Taurus, and in aspect to Venus, Venus receives Mars as a guest and supports. When two planets are in mutual reception, they are each in a sign that the other rules or are in dignity and develop a supportive relationship.

Rectification: When we don't have an individual's birth time, some talented astrologers can rectify the chart by using many major events in a person's life to work backward. The process is complex but can produce a useful chart.

Retrograde: If you observe the planets from the Sun, all the planets orbit in the same direction and none ever appear to back up. But from our perspective here on Earth, because of the difference between our orbit and theirs, all the planets (except for the Sun and Moon) occasionally appear to stand still and then dance backward against the backdrop of the zodiac. When a planet retrogrades, events symbolized by that planet won't go as they normally do. A retrograde planet signals you to review, fix gaps, reconsider, and consolidate what you've learned before proceeding into the next chapter.

Right ascension: A heavenly version of terrestrial longitude that measures positions east or west of the equator. Astrologers developed many tools to try to define the space around our globe because this was a tricky thing to do. Right ascension measures the distance of a celestial object from zero degrees of Aries along the plane of the celestial equator—the plane created by the Earthly equator projected out into space.

Rising sign: The sign rising over the eastern horizon at the moment the chart was cast; a.k.a. the ascendant.

S

Soft aspects: The trine and sextile create a comfortable and flowing energy between two planets; they point toward easy rapport between the parts of our lives symbolized by those planets. Too many soft aspects imply that one can be adverse to the work necessary to live up to one's potential. Too few and life can feel like a lot of hard work.

Sabian symbol: Each of the 360 degrees of the zodiac has a symbol, phrase, or image to go with it, which implies some important characteristics about that degree. In 1925 the astrologer Marc Edmund Jones recorded as a clairvoyant friend, Elsie Wheeler, channeled these images. Several other astrologers have expanded these images, or came up with their own, to further this understanding.

Secondary progressions: We imprint the pattern the planets make during the first few months after our birth. They sketch out the major landscape of our life's progress. We then live out that pattern, with a lot of choice about how, throughout our life. Secondary progressions map this pattern at roughly the rate of a day to a year; 30 days old symbolically maps your thirtieth year.

Sect: Just like many people's dispositions, some planets are more comfortable and stronger in the daytime, others at night. If the Sun is above the horizon, our chart is a daylight or diurnal chart. If the Sun is below the horizon, it's a nighttime or nocturnal chart. Whether a planet is in sect is considered an important dignity/debility in traditional astrology; although all planets are still active, planets in sect, in their favorite time of the day, take a step forward into the foreground with strength and clarity while those out of sect take a step back. Each team has a luminary plus a benefic and malefic planet. Mercury, as usual, is mercurial, and changes depending upon circumstances.

> **Diurnal:** Sun, Jupiter, Saturn.

> **Nocturnal:** Moon, Venus, Mars

Semi-decile: A minor positive aspect of 18 degrees.

Semi-quintile: A minor positive aspect of 36 degrees.

Semi-sextile: A minor aspect similar in gift and challenge to the quincunx, 30 degrees, or one sign apart.

Semi-square: A relatively minor uncomfortable aspect of 45 degrees.

Separator: A planet that is separating, or moving away from an exact aspect, an aspect of fading influence. In a natal chart it may refer to a story that began another life and/or began in the family before the person was born. It refers to an event that has already occurred.

Sesqui-quadrate: A minor challenging aspect of 135 degrees.

Sextile: A soft aspect between two points roughly 60 degrees apart, usually between two planets of the same polarity. The sextile is a buddy aspect. Like Butch Cassidy and the Sundance Kid or Thelma and Louise, these two planets egg each other on, and back each other up, but may not give each other the hard news.

Short ascension signs: Capricorn, Aquarius, Pisces, Aries, Taurus, and Gemini. One or more of these signs may be intercepted between houses in the northern hemisphere chart.

Sidereal Astrology: From the Latin word for "star," *sider*, the term sidereal deals with movement in relationship to the distant stars. Most of Western astrology is based on the tropical system, which defines the zodiac by the Earth's relationship to the Sun and uses the solstices and equinox as turning points. Sidereal astrology is used by both the Vedic system and Western sidereal astrology and follows the fixed stars and constellations instead. These two systems developed their nomenclature together several thousand years ago but mean different concepts when they talk about signs. Because our whole solar system is moving through the galaxy, and the galaxy through the universe, the two systems drifted apart by about 1.4 degrees every century. Both systems work within their own internally consistent patterns.

Sidereal time: Our day is 24 hours, the time it takes for the Earth to rotate and face the Sun again in the same position. The Earth spins on its axis in only 23 hours, 56 minutes, and 4.1 seconds, which is one sidereal day. We need those extra 4 minutes to return to face the Sun because the Sun has also traveled 2.5 million km that day. The Earth is in the same place relative to the fixed stars at the end of a sidereal day, but not in the same place related to the Sun. This little difference gives us the changing skies through the seasons and makes astrological calculations intriguingly challenging.

Significator: A planet in charge. The planet that rules the ascendant in natal astrology. Horary astrology answers a question by drawing up a chart for the moment the question is posed; here the significator is the planet that rules the house governing the question.

Solar arc progressions: The Sun moves forward about 1 degree a day. In solar arc progressions all the planets are asked to follow the Sun and so move forward 1 degree for every year of a person's life. If, for example, your Mars is at 0 degrees of Leo, and your Sun is at 23 degrees of Leo, then when you are 23 years old, your solar arc Mars would conjunct your natal Sun, and you might need to do something extra with your energy that year, take on a healthy challenge and use the positive edge of Mars.

Solar return: Many happy returns . . . A solar return chart is made for the moment the Sun returns to its exact place at the moment of your birth and offers you a snapshot of the year ahead. Astrologers use variations on this theme, each with its own adherents. Some astrologers choose to do this for the place of birth; others draw the chart for where the Sun will return for the person's location on their birthday. Some use precession-corrected timing and others don't. Each chart offers a different view.

Solstice: From *sol* (the Sun) + *sistere* ("stand still"). Cancer and Capricorn begin at this point on the Sun cycle when the Sun is at its farthest point from the equator, Cancer to the north, Capricorn to the south. Here in the North we observe the Sun setting farther and farther south each day through the fall, then around December 21, it will rise and set at the same point, appearing to stand still for three days before it starts to move north again. Note that many mythologies tell a story of a deity who dies and after three days rises again from the dead.

Superior planets: This term doesn't mean they are better, but they are planets whose orbit lies beyond that of the Earth, farther from the Sun: Mars, Jupiter, Saturn, Uranus, Neptune, Pluto.

Swift in motion: A planet that is moving faster than its average motion.

Synastry: The art of comparing two charts together to understand their relationship dynamics. One method is to create two wheels with each person's planets in a ring on the outside of the other, as if that person was a permanent transit to your chart.

Syzygy: From a Greek term that means "yoked together," syzygy is created when three or more planets align in a rough straight line, either by conjunction or opposition.

Southern signs: When the Sun is south of the equator, it is traveling through Libra, Scorpio, Sagittarius, Capricorn, Aquarius, it is traveling south of the equator.

Square: A strong, challenging aspect between two celestial bodies of 90 degrees, at a right angle. Two planets of the same modality and similar degree square one another.

Stationary: A planet stations, as if it is holding still against the backdrop of the zodiac, as it slows down to turn retrograde (see *retrograde*). The Sun and Moon never station. Mercury stationary can be experienced as more difficult than Mercury retrograde—the Mercury archetype likes to move.

Stellium: A group of three or more planets close together in one sign or house. Like underlining a trait three times, a stellium intensifies the characteristics of that sign or house. With several planets close together, powerful as they are, it can be hard to understand how to kick them into gear. Develop the skills of the sign and house opposite it to balance a stellium and unpack its contents.

Succedent: Houses which follow, or succeed, a cardinal house, a.k.a. fixed houses, the middle house in each quadrant, which are the second, fifth, eighth, and eleventh.

T

Table of houses: You need this to calculate a chart by hand, which, while no longer needed regularly in this age of computers, is necessary to become a professional astrologer. The table of houses is a giant book in tiny print that gives the signs and degrees on the cusps of the houses at the appropriate sidereal time and earthly latitude of the birth, all needed to construct an accurate natal chart. One of the many reasons why computers have expanded the field of astrology and brought insight into astrology from nonmathematical people.

Terms: Also known as *bounds*. Traditional astrology has a complex map of rulership within the signs, and so planets gain a minor essential dignity by being in certain allotted places or degrees.

Tertiary progressions: A forecasting tool (see *progressions*). Secondary progressions look at the correlation between the days in the first few months of your life, and years afterward, and are therefore based on the Sun. Tertiary progressions are less used than secondary, based on the lunar cycle, and equate one lunar month to a year.

Traditional astrology: Astrological history started around four thousand years ago in Chaldea and Babylonia, became more formalized around 600 B.C.E. with the systemization of the zodiac, and evolved as astrologers refined prediction and psychological correspondences in the Greek golden age. Astrology, science, and philosophy were still nurtured in Afghanistan, India, and the Middle East during the Dark Ages, when they were buried in Europe. Our awareness of the solar system expanded as Uranus was discovered in 1781, followed over the next two centuries with Neptune, Pluto, and the asteroids. Modern astrology utilizes the outer planets, asteroids, and other phenomena and became more psychological, but as we expanded its toolbox, much of the pragmatic exactness of traditional astrology got lost. In the last few decades many ancient texts have been translated and reintroduced a rich library of careful traditional techniques to the body of astrology, which is why traditional astrology is new again.

Transit: The planets are always moving through the solar system. As they move, they interact with one another forming geometric relationship aspects, which are the transits of the minute, the mundane transits, and create the astrological weather of the moment. Transiting planets interact with our natal chart and progressions like fingers on harp strings. When a transiting planet waltzes through our houses or interacts geometrically with a planet in our natal chart, it strikes that chord, energizes it, and reverberates for a while afterward. The effect of that reverberation depends on the nature of the aspect, whether it is supportive or challenging, the nature of the actor, the planet transiting, the nature of the planet in our chart being acted upon, and how we choose to respond to that signal.

Trine: A strongly supportive aspect between two planets roughly 120 degrees apart, usually from the same element—fire to fire or water to water. Trines encourage these parts of our life and soul to work together; they give us ease and talent, help us amalgamate our skills, but do not necessarily imply strength.

Triplicity: Also known as *trigon*, a description of the three signs within one element—fire, Earth, air, or water. If a planet is in a triplicity in which it rules a sign, it is a bit stronger and more direct, a minor essential dignity.

Tropical signs: Cancer and Capricorn. The Tropic of Cancer and the Tropic of Capricorn are latitude lines on our global maps at approximately 26 degrees north and south, defined by the path of the Sun at its farthest northern solstice, beginning the sign of Cancer, and the path at the southern Solstice, marking the beginning of the sign Capricorn. In between these two lines are the tropics.

U

Under the beams: When a planet is within 17 degrees of the Sun by some astrologers, more specifically between 8 degrees and 15 degrees of the Sun, the planet is no longer visible to our naked eye, and though that planet will affect the nature of the Sun's expression, it may have trouble expressing itself as an individual force, and so the planet is considered weaker. This concept is used more in horary astrology than in natal. From 8 to 0 degrees is considered combust the Sun (see *combust*).

V

Vigintile: A minor positive aspect of 18 degrees.

Void of course: A planet is considered *void of course* when it completes the last major aspect to another planet before it changes signs. A void of course planet may have an aimless or wandering quality until it changes signs, as if it's taking a break and not really relating to other planets for a bit, a good time to reflect, review, and reorganize. If the Moon is void of course in the chart of an event, to some it implies that nothing will come of the matter. There is a disagreement among astrologers on the strength of this effect, because the planet is always shifting toward another aspect in the future. Observe it for yourself and see how you react to the void of course planet. In mundane astrology the void of course time can be a time when it is hard to keep a meeting focused or hard to come to decisions. Extra effort may need to be made to bring these decisions to fruition.

W

Water signs: Cancer, Scorpio, and Pisces.

Z

Zenith: A point directly overhead.

Zodiac: A circle of 360 degrees, divided into 12 equal sectors of 30 degrees each that are the astrology signs. For the difference between Western and Eastern concepts of the zodiac, see the preface.

RESOURCES

Casey, Caroline. *Making the Gods Work for You: The Astrological Language of the Psyche.* New York: Harmony, 1999.

George, Demetra. *Astrology and the Authentic Self: Integrating Traditional and Modern Astrology to Uncover the Essence of the Birth Chart.* Ibis Press, 2008.

George, Demetra and Douglas Bloch. *Asteroid Goddesses: The Mythology, Psychology and Astrology of the Re-Emerging Feminine.* Newburyport, MA: Nicolas-Hays, Inc, 2003.

Guttman, Arielle. *Venus Star Rising: A New Cosmology for the Twenty-First Century.* Sophia Venus Productions, 2011.

Guttman, Arielle and Kenneth Johnson. *Mythic Astrology: Archetypes in the Horoscope.* Sophia Venus Productions, 2016.

Jones, Mark. *Healing the Soul: Pluto, Uranus and the Lunar Nodes.* Portland, OR: Raven Dreams Press, 2011.

Sparkly Kat, Alice. *Postcolonial Astrology: Reading the Planets Through Capital, Power, and Labor.* Berkeley, CA: North Atlantic Books, 2021.

Spiller, Jan. *Astrology for the Soul.* New York: Bantam, 1997.

ACKNOWLEDGMENTS

I have had the joy of befriending and working with some wonderful astrologers over the years. I dedicate this book to them all. Thank you all for your investigations, collegiality, and sincere interest in making astrology a valuable and integrous field. Thank you to my great companion, Dr. Wren Walker Robbins, for walking with me. Great gratitude to my adult progenies—Vanessa Shaughnessy, Max Rowntree, and Jess Mckeen—and all your families, for heart and context. I've learned so much from you all and from watching your charts as you grew. Thank you to my amazing *Starcodes* illustrator, Lucas Lua De Souza. I love my tattoo from your work. Thank you to my talented webmaster, Cee Lippens, and most wholeheartedly, thank you to the nurturing and brilliant team at Hay House for supporting me through this journey.

ABOUT THE AUTHOR

Heather Roan Robbins, M.Th., is a ceremonialist, counselor, and a choice-oriented astrologer with 40-plus years' experience and an active online international practice. Her father, Walter Gottschalk, was an abstract mathematician who invented a field of topology, topological dynamics. Her mother was a psychiatric nurse. The family joke was "Put them in a blender, and you get an astrologer." Heather has lived in New England, New York City, New Mexico, and Minnesota, and now lives in Montana. For 30 years she has written *Starcodes*, a weekly column by day and not by sign, and for the We'Moon calendar. She has authored the books *Moon Wisdom* and *Everyday Palmistry*, two children's books through CICO Books, and the *Starcodes Astro Oracle* through Hay House, which has now been translated into 11 languages. She is also an Ordained Interfaith and Druid–grade member of OBOD, the Order of Bards, Ovates, and Druids. Find her online at **roanrobbins.com**.

ABOUT THE ILLUSTRATOR

Lucas Lua De Souza is a tattoo artist from Brazil who currently lives in beautiful Melbourne, Australia. He is the illustrator of *Starcodes Astro Oracle*. Lucas grew up with a love of drawing and would spend hours sketching on the pages of his schoolbooks during his spare time. His life changed forever when his mom gave him his first tattoo gun on his birthday. Find him online at **lucaslua.com**.

Hay House Titles of Related Interest

We hope you enjoyed this Hay House book. If you'd like to receive our online catalog featuring additional information on Hay House books and products, or if you'd like to find out more about the Hay Foundation, please contact:

Hay House LLC, P.O. Box 5100, Carlsbad, CA 92018-5100
(760) 431-7695 or (800) 654-5126
www.hayhouse.com® • www.hayfoundation.org

———

Published in Australia by:
Hay House Australia Publishing Pty Ltd
18/36 Ralph St., Alexandria NSW 2015
Phone: +61 (02) 9669 4299
www.hayhouse.com.au

Published in the United Kingdom by:
Hay House UK Ltd
The Sixth Floor, Watson House,
54 Baker Street, London W1U 7BU
Phone: +44 (0) 203 927 7290
www.hayhouse.co.uk

Published in India by:
Hay House Publishers (India) Pvt Ltd
Muskaan Complex, Plot No. 3,
B-2, Vasant Kunj, New Delhi 110 070
Phone: +91 11 41761620
www.hayhouse.co.in

———

Access New Knowledge.
Anytime. Anywhere.

Learn and evolve at your own pace
with the world's leading experts.

www.hayhouseU.com